D1000399

MATT MAYBERRY

CULTURE

IS THE

WAY

HOW LEADERS AT EVERY LEVEL
BUILD AN ORGANIZATION
FOR SPEED, IMPACT, AND EXCELLENCE

WILEY

Copyright © 2023 by Matt Mayberry. All rights reserved.

Published by John Wiley & Sons, Inc., Hoboken, New Jersey.
Published simultaneously in Canada.

No part of this publication may be reproduced, stored in a retrieval system, or transmitted in any form or by any means, electronic, mechanical, photocopying, recording, scanning, or otherwise, except as permitted under Section 107 or 108 of the 1976 United States Copyright Act, without either the prior written permission of the Publisher, or authorization through payment of the appropriate per-copy fee to the Copyright Clearance Center, Inc., 222 Rosewood Drive, Danvers, MA 01923, (978) 750-8400, fax (978) 750-4470, or on the web at www.copyright.com. Requests to the Publisher for permission should be addressed to the Permissions Department, John Wiley & Sons, Inc., 111 River Street, Hoboken, NJ 07030, (201) 748-6011, fax (201) 748-6008, or online at http://www.wiley.com/go/permission.

Trademarks: Wiley and the Wiley logo are trademarks or registered trademarks of John Wiley & Sons, Inc. and/or its affiliates in the United States and other countries and may not be used without written permission. All other trademarks are the property of their respective owners. John Wiley & Sons, Inc. is not associated with any product or vendor mentioned in this book.

Limit of Liability/Disclaimer of Warranty: While the publisher and author have used their best efforts in preparing this book, they make no representations or warranties with respect to the accuracy or completeness of the contents of this book and specifically disclaim any implied warranties of merchantability or fitness for a particular purpose. No warranty may be created or extended by sales representatives or written sales materials. The advice and strategies contained herein may not be suitable for your situation. You should consult with a professional where appropriate. Further, readers should be aware that websites listed in this work may have changed or disappeared between when this work was written and when it is read. Neither the publisher nor authors shall be liable for any loss of profit or any other commercial damages, including but not limited to special, incidental, consequential, or other damages.

For general information on our other products and services or for technical support, please contact our Customer Care Department within the United States at (800) 762-2974, outside the United States at (317) 572-3993 or fax (317) 572-4002.

Wiley also publishes its books in a variety of electronic formats. Some content that appears in print may not be available in electronic formats. For more information about Wiley products, visit our web site at **www.wiley.com**.

Library of Congress Cataloging-in-Publication Data:

Names: Mayberry, Matt, 1987– author.
Title: Culture is the way : how leaders at every level build an
  organization for speed, impact, and excellence / Matt Mayberry.
Description: Hoboken, New Jersey : Wiley, [2023] | Includes index.
Identifiers: LCCN 2022035758 (print) | LCCN 2022035759 (ebook) | ISBN
  9781119913658 (hardback) | ISBN 9781119913672 (adobe pdf) | ISBN
  9781119913665 (epub)
Subjects: LCSH: Corporate culture. | Leadership.
Classification: LCC HD58.7 .M3797 2023 (print) | LCC HD58.7 (ebook) | DDC
  302.3/5—dc23/eng/20221108
LC record available at https://lccn.loc.gov/2022035758
LC ebook record available at https://lccn.loc.gov/2022035759

Cover Design and Image: Wiley

SKY10039736_120922

Contents

Author's Note

Some incidents, events, and dialogues are drawn from my imagination and are not to be construed as verbatim, even though they are all based on real people, results, businesses, conversations, and events. Some places and companies have been changed, and many of the names have been changed, along with some features and characteristics, to preserve their anonymity.

Figure List

Acknowledgments

Writing a book is never a solo act, and this book was no exception. Finishing this book and completing the manuscript would not have been possible without the special people in my life.

Thank you to my wonderful wife, Aubry, for being so patient with me.

Katie Kotchman, my agent, has always been one of my biggest supporters. Thank you for listening to my crazy ideas and encouraging me.

I'd like to express my gratitude to Wiley, my publisher, for not only believing in but also showing great excitement for this book. Richard Narramore, my editor, was instrumental from the beginning.

Thank you, Donna Peerce, for your contribution, productive discussions, and executing every minor detail.

This book wouldn't have been possible without the help of all of the business leaders who allowed me to interview them and took time out of their busy schedules to help with the production of this book. I greatly benefited from the information you shared with me as well as your leadership.

Each and every client, as well as the organizations and leaders who entrust me with your most valuable asset, your people, means the world to me. My work certainly doesn't feel like work. I am so fortunate for each and every opportunity, relationship formed, and your partnership.

CHAPTER 1

Is Culture Powerful? Ask a Football Coach

Customers will never love a company until the employees love it first.

— Simon Sinek, author of *Start with Why*

Football was the first "team" that taught me about culture. As a football player at Indiana University, I first discovered the extraordinary power and capacity of culture. Terry Hoeppner, my head coach at the time, was one of the most remarkable individuals I have ever had the privilege of knowing. Coach Hep, as we called him, was a special, inspiring, and passionate man whom I wrote extensively about in my first book, *Winning Plays*.

We were the laughingstock of the Big Ten Conference for football when Coach Hep first arrived at Indiana. We were known more for throwing one of the best tailgate parties in the conference than for providing an electrifying atmosphere to watch Big Ten college football.

The energy and enthusiasm for the future of Indiana Football began to shift after Coach Hep arrived and took charge of our team. Coach Hep had an almost magical aura about him, and when people were with him, they felt an openness, kindness, and friendliness. He was convinced that our football program had the potential to be great one day, and he acted accordingly. He continually talked to us about changing the culture of Indiana Football and setting new expectations for us as players. Everything he did, whether it was sharing his favorite poems or quotes before every team meeting, constantly breaking down the program's future vision, or encouraging and coaching us up at every opportunity, was geared toward changing the program's old beliefs.

Coach Hep died from a lingering illness during my sophomore year. When he passed away, I don't think there was a dry eye in Indiana because he was truly one of the greats. Everyone was left with fond, heartfelt memories and an indelible impression of him.

Our football team dedicated the upcoming season in his honor. We carried his passion, vision, and spirit with us on the field and ended up going to a Bowl game that year. This was our first Bowl game appearance in fourteen years. Yes, you read that correctly. *Fourteen years!* We didn't have an extreme upgrade in talent. So, it wasn't the talent on the roster that helped us break the fourteen-year curse of making it to a Bowl game. And we had the same schedule of facing some of the best teams in college football, including perennial powerhouses like Ohio State and Michigan. So, it wasn't because of an easier schedule and weaker opponents.

Simply, it was due to the dedication and leadership of one man who worked diligently day and night to alter the perception and culture of Indiana Football. Coach Hep instilled in us a passionate culture with new mindsets, visions, beliefs, and behaviors that we carried over onto the football field. That is the power of a passionate leader who prioritizes culture-building and how it can have a profound impact on every aspect of our lives, whether in sports, business, society, or education.

Success Leaves Clues

I learned so many valuable lessons from playing the game of football. From the time I started playing as a little kid, all the way through high school, college, and eventually the NFL, the life lessons accumulated from the game have benefited my life in so many ways.

Over time, I realized that the same characteristics that distinguish the best football teams are also required to succeed in business. A strong commitment to excellence, an emphasis on teamwork, practicing like a champion every day, and perseverance in the face of adversity are a few of these traits. Those same characteristics have been invaluable not only in helping me build my own thriving consulting and speaking business, but also in transforming the organizational and cultural performance of many leading companies.

Adopting some of the key learnings from the game of football and implementing certain aspects of them in the business world is now a large part of the culture work that I conduct for organizations. I am very passionate about the idea that all business leaders should research their favorite sports coaches. Some business leaders and managers clearly understand the power of culture, but most allow it to become a flavor of the month rather than developing the consistency required to build a great one. Even if you aren't a sports fan but currently lead or manage others, I believe there is tremendous insight to be gained from studying the best teams and coaches in athletics.

Great coaches understand the power of culture better than anyone else. In June 2021, *The Athletic* magazine published an excellent article about how some of the best coaches prioritize building a strong team culture and just how important it is to their team's success.[1]

Joe Smith, an *Athletic* staff writer, spoke with Golden State Warriors Head Coach Steve Kerr, Alabama Football Head Coach Nick Saban, Tampa Bay Buccaneers Head Coach Bruce Arians, and Los Angeles Angels Manager Joe Maddon. Smith wrote in the article, "Turns out, *culture* isn't a buzzword to them. It's bedrock."

There is no telling what could happen if more business leaders had the same perspective on culture as some of the greatest sports coaches. Not only do I believe we would build more workplaces that don't struggle to attract top talent, but I also believe we would see more companies play a significant role in making the world a better place and positively shaping every aspect of their employees' lives.

Let's examine three key lessons from great sports coaches that business leaders at all levels can apply as we move forward on the culture-building journey.

1. Develop a burning desire to improve culture.
2. Generate and bring positive energy daily.
3. Don't just *manage* people, *coach* your people.

Develop a Burning Desire to Improve Culture

I have never yet met a great coach who did not have a burning desire to improve their team's culture. Whether the team had a fantastic or a terrible season the previous year, their passion and desire for cultural improvement never wavered. It's something I've always admired about the great coaches I've had throughout my football career. Every day, they poured everything they had into building the culture. They linked it to every teaching point, whether it was on the recruiting trail, during a game, in practice, or even while watching film.

You can't just be interested in creating a great culture. Leaders who are committed outperform leaders who are only "mildly" interested. Most coaches are obsessed with culture because a mentor or another coach taught them its value. For example, Nick Saban, the head coach of the Alabama Crimson Tide and one of the greatest college football coaches of all time, said that he learned about the importance of culture from Bill Belichick, the legendary head coach of the New England Patriots.

Make it a priority as a leader to learn from other leaders who are exceptional builders of culture. Whether those leaders are from within or outside of your industry, study them, and become fanatical about following the way they utilize cultural best practices.

Generate and Bring Positive Energy Daily

As a leader, you are directly responsible for generating energy and setting the tone for the rest of the organization daily. I am continually astounded by how many leaders vastly underestimate the value of the energy they convey to their workforce on a daily, weekly, and monthly basis. I'm not suggesting you change or modify your personality, but this is something that all great sports coaches understand and intentionally practice. The daily energy you inject into the organization either fuels the execution of your culture or impedes the growth and development of your efforts.

There are going to be many things that happen throughout the course of a day that you will have no control over. Don't let a *controllable event*—something we do have control over—be up for questioning. Building a healthy, positive, and thriving culture is extremely hard work. There is nothing easy about it. If you are going to alter the mindsets, behaviors, and attitudes of those whom you lead, it is going to demand a certain level of bold, positive energy from you as the leader of an organization.

When Coach Hep began to gradually alter the culture of the football team, it was his daily demonstration of positive energy, rather than the words that came out of his mouth, that had the greatest impact. He cared, and it was obvious. For successful change initiatives not only to work, but also to keep going forward, positive energy must be generated throughout the whole organization.

Don't Just *Manage* People, *Coach* Your People

You must lead the way, manage the process, and then relentlessly coach your people. Ask any current or former athlete about the best coach they've ever had. Chances are that they will tell you that their best coach did a whole lot more than establish the team's vision or oversee the day-to-day operations of the team. They will almost certainly tell you that their lives were profoundly changed, both personally and professionally, because of how that coach brought out the best in them. That coach was probably tough on them, but it was only because they wanted the best for their team and the player.

Their toughness and drive for excellence were never misinterpreted as micromanagement or toxic behavior because the players knew their coach genuinely cared about them as individuals. The best coaches in sports, as well as the most effective business leaders who successfully drive transformation across entire organizations, devote a significant amount of time to coaching. They are out in the market showing, leading, and coaching the way forward.

Coaches on the best athletic teams teach and coach their players not only on the techniques necessary to win on the field or court, but also on the behaviors and mindset needed to advance the culture. Even though when you watch a sporting event on television you may see the coaches screaming and constantly yelling, behind the scenes they spend more time listening than talking.

The Larger Room

Whenever I arrive in any city to speak at a major conference, whether it's in front of hundreds or thousands, I like to prepare by acquainting myself with what I deem as the "larger room." The evening before my talk, or predawn, I will often go to the conference room where my keynote is being held and step out onto the stage. I look out at the empty audience, chairs organized in rows or around tables, a table set up in the back of the room where my books will be featured, and I envision the throngs of people who will be in the audience and start thinking deeply about the impact that I want to create.

I have already spent hours researching this company's culture, so I'm prepared to connect with them and deliver meaningful value to help them exactly where they are.

I walk around the stage, encompassing as much of it as I can. Then I imagine the audience enthusiastically clapping, because I believe they will be inspired to enter their own larger rooms to take their organization's performance to the next level.

As a leader and manager of people, each morning you should be awakening in a larger room, too. This larger room is simply a more expansive vision and heightened perspective of opportunity.

If you close your eyes, you will see in that larger room an open space that is big enough to fill an expanded set of organizational excellence possibilities. Things like:

- Revenue and profit growth.
- Market share increase.
- Trust among stakeholders.
- Profitability.

- Customer satisfaction and fulfillment.
- Employee commitment and loyalty.
- Inspiring and collaborative leadership.
- Purpose.
- Innovation.
- Alignment.
- Revolution. And a lot more.

At first, this larger room might feel too big, too void of business syntax, too overwhelming, too empty, but think of it this way. It's providing you with an open space for envisioning, creating, and developing innovative ways to move forward in your company and with your teams in a constantly changing business world. So, you can become and achieve *more*.

Let's face it. The pace of business is accelerating, and leaders must remain cognizant of the ways to succeed in a new world of work and the new opportunities for growth and change. Instead of fighting the tides of change, we must embrace them. After all, do you want to be stranded in an outdated set of possibilities that houses an old, myopic, smaller way of thinking and doing, or do you want to eagerly step into a bigger, brighter room that presents a more profitable future?

I'd like to remind you that when you wake up and enter this larger room of expanded possibilities, take with you all that you have learned in the past, but remain open to new, extraordinary ways to lead and make an impact as a leader.

There is no doubt in my mind that culture is the way to move forward in this larger room.

Let me briefly explain. Since 2020 and the Coronavirus pandemic, we have experienced new challenges and have seen rapidly changing environments that have dislodged us from our stagnant ways of thinking and behaving. Our former beliefs about business culture, how we care for our employees, how we work, and how we lead will most likely not serve us today as we move forward in the pursuit of continued growth and excellence.

All leaders and people managers face an arduous array of fluctuating challenges. They face trying tests like creating and building organizations that can sustain economic downturns, potential world wars, pandemics, AI, and legislative uncertainty, all the while maintaining long-term viability and gaining a competitive advantage.

When I talk about waking up in a larger room, this is what I mean. In spite of all the challenges, this larger room offers an expansive and enduring vision that allows us to see endless opportunities.

Leading Boldly into the Future

We must face facts. It's a bold new world that requires bold new leadership.

Only 20% of global workers are actively engaged in their work. The global economy is driven by the workers making up this global minority. They add tremendous value, not only to the organizations for which they work but also to the communities in which they live. The other 80% are merely going through the motions. In some instances, those that fall into the 80% may even despise their current workplace and the manager they report to.[2]

Companies of all sizes have an extraordinary opportunity to change the narrative right now. And each time the narrative is altered for the better, the world is more susceptible to transformation and advancement. I realize this is a bold claim. I mean, when was the last time we thought of companies as having the power and potential to not only do good in the world, but also make the world a better and improved place?

Many of you may not have given much thought to improving the world through better leadership and creating better workplace cultures. For the past few years, however, I've been convinced that this stance is beginning to shift. Organizations can and do have a positive effect on the world around them. Leadership and managers at every level can make a significant contribution to making the world a better place.

As you will learn throughout *Culture Is the Way*, it all starts with the organizational cultures that leaders build and how boldly they lead into the future. With each bold step forward, we can transform not only business performance but also the world around us and the communities that we serve.

Do business leaders always get it right? Of course not. There will be plenty of challenges on the journey ahead, and mistakes will be made. Priorities will change, but the pace of business will not slow down. Our attention span will most likely fluctuate, and we will continually be pulled in a million different directions. However, when our organizational values are deeply meaningful and paired with wisdom, purpose, and action, when they are embedded into daily behaviors, we move one step closer to creating a thriving culture, and when we do so, we bring our entire workforce into that larger room of greatness.

When we lead boldly into the future and develop those within our organizations to become a more well-rounded and better version of themselves, we move one step closer to making a bigger impact, and our room expands to an even *larger* room of possibilities.

Let me give you another example of why I am certain of this. In a survey conducted by the public relations firm Edelman Trust Barometer, survey participants said that they have more trust and faith in their employers than they do in their governments.[3]

That means there is more hope and opportunity for leaders and organizations around the world than perhaps ever before. We can debate the survey results for hours, but the truth is that leaders and organizations have a once-in-a-lifetime opportunity to rewrite history and create a much bigger and better future.

Many people don't view companies as being responsible for positively shaping the lives of employees. In fact, most employees are reminded of what their parents and grandparents used to preach: "Get a great education, get a job to pay your bills, and work hard." Sure, this still rings true to a certain degree, but it's becoming more stagnant every day because the workforce has changed in the twenty-first century and a new set of competencies and capabilities are required to have a career that prospers.

On the enterprise side, most organizations have been known to only care about increasing profits, building a sustainable business model, and delivering exceptional results every year for customers and shareholders. While these general assumptions are not wrong, there is certainly a lot more that is needed to win in the constantly evolving dynamics of business.

Employees demand more from their employers now than at any other time in history. And if employers do not deliver, employees are ready to leave. We've all seen signs in front of local businesses, restaurants, and factories: "We're hiring!" "Help wanted!"

We've wondered how there can be so many open jobs when nearly every employer seems to be offering better pay, benefits, and even handsome signing bonuses. The government's employment report reveals what has occurred: In the latter half of 2021, well over 20 million people quit their jobs. Some have been referring to it as the "Big Quit," and others have called it the "Great Resignation."[4]

What impact does culture have on talent? When it comes to attracting new and aspiring top talent, a company's culture is critical. In a survey conducted by Glassdoor, 77% of respondents indicated that the company's culture would play a significant role in their decision to apply for a job. Millennials in the United States said that work culture is more important than salary (65%) compared to those aged 45 and older (52%). A similar pattern was seen outside of the United States in the United Kingdom (66% vs. 52%). Some 89% of adults polled said it was vital for employers to have a clear mission and purpose. Glassdoor's research shows that a company's pay and benefits are not the only factor in attracting talent, and that the company's culture may be just as important, if not more so.[5]

"A common misperception among many employers today is that pay and work–life balance are among the top factors driving employee satisfaction," said Dr. Andrew Chamberlain, Glassdoor's chief economist. "We find little support for this notion in Glassdoor data. Instead, employers looking to boost hiring and employee retention efforts should prioritize building strong company culture and value systems, amplifying the quality and visibility of their senior leadership teams, and offering clear, exciting career opportunities to employees."

Not only does culture matter when it comes to attracting talent, but it is also important when it comes to retaining talent. According to the same survey, 65% said their company's culture was the major reason for staying.

With competition intensifying in nearly every industry and external threats increasing daily, enterprises will struggle to compete and win by doing what they have always done in the absence of a new focus on culture.

The Power of Culture

Overall, culture wields enormous power. It is the deciding factor that not only can create an incredibly dynamic, innovative workplace but also drive extraordinary levels of execution in the marketplace. Culture is the way forward if we are to embrace this expanded set of possibilities and build an outstanding organization that serves a purpose greater than just profit. And one more thing. When I say culture, I don't mean company perks like unlimited vacation time or sleep pods on every floor of the company's headquarters or some cute phrase that leaders throw around every now and then in the hopes of making employees or shareholders happy. In the following chapters, we will define culture in depth and examine how it can help an organization succeed.

When it comes to culture, one of the most glaring issues is that far too many leaders do not recognize it as one of their greatest competitive advantages. And for the leaders who do see it as a competitive advantage, their daily actions often contradict this. Culture should not be an afterthought that is left to the HR department or a separate project that will be taken care of when business slows down.

The best leaders not only see culture as a major organizational imperative but also put culture at the forefront of everything they do. "I came to see, in my time at IBM, that culture isn't just one aspect of the game; it is the game," former IBM CEO Lou Gerstner said.

> *Your strategy can be stolen and copied by the competition. They can try to mimic your sales process and clone the vast majority of your company's daily operations. The culture you create is something that no one, including your competitors, can take away or imitate.*

Yes, culture is powerful, and it absolutely has an impact on business performance, particularly when management is focused on integrating all their culture work into every aspect of their business. A Harvard University study found that companies with a strong and healthy culture experienced a 756% increase in net income compared to those with a weaker culture.[6] I don't know about you, but even if that number is slightly inflated, it still represents a staggering level of growth in the type of business impact that developing a winning culture can have on an organization.

Garry Ridge, Chairman and CEO of WD-40 Company, told me that building culture is a sacred responsibility that has paid off handsomely in terms of business performance. The company's sales have quadrupled over the past two decades. Furthermore, their market cap increased from $250 million to nearly $2.5 billion. WD-40 Company's annual compounded growth rate of total shareholder return has been 15% over the last two decades. According to Garry, the company's "tribal culture" is their secret sauce and unquestionably their greatest advantage. What accounts for WD-40 Company's exceptional employee engagement survey results and astounding market performance? Garry stated that everything boils down to the *Four Pillars of the Fearless Tribe*. The four pillars are: care, candor, accountability, and responsibility.[7]

What about the business repercussions of ignoring culture and having a toxic workplace environment? SHRM published some startling data and research on the costly consequences of toxic cultures in 2019. Over a five-year period, organizations lost $223 billion due to employee turnover caused by a poor workplace culture; 49% of employees were contemplating leaving their current jobs due to a negative workplace culture. In the past five years, one-fifth of employees left their positions due to company culture.[8] And these figures were released in 2019. I'd wager that these figures have gotten worse over time. Culture has extraordinary power, but it can be quite costly if not taken seriously.

As a keynote speaker, executive coach, and management consultant, I've had the privilege of traveling the world for the past decade, working with game-changing business leaders and some of the world's most prestigious organizations. In my work as a consultant and advisor, I have the unique opportunity to witness cultural and organizational transformations that even those on the inside of an organization once thought were impossible to achieve. I've seen firsthand what can happen when an organization and its leaders begin to ruthlessly build and passionately prioritize culture.

Why This Book and Why Now?

The world felt like it came crashing down on us in March 2020, when the Coronavirus pandemic completely upended how we work, how we lead, and how some businesses compete and succeed in the marketplace.

Some companies were able to successfully adapt and continue moving forward, but the reality is that many companies struggled to find success back then and continue to do so now.

In the past, the word "culture" was often used in the corporate world as a hot commodity, popularized by Silicon Valley. When leaders were told that improving their workplace culture should be a priority, they often rolled their eyes.

Everything changed overnight all over the world because of the COVID-19 crisis. Business, as we've known it for the past century, died. The old, painfully outdated management styles were completely turned upside down, and the importance of workplace culture became more important than ever.

These shifts brought to light by the pandemic were not temporary. They're not going anywhere. That is what compelled me to write this book. In the midst of a pandemic, the companies that were able to succeed and even advance their mission stood out from the companies that struggled, and for the most part, it was because of their culture.

Please don't take this the wrong way, but I must be honest. A small part of me is happy that the pandemic has emphasized the significance of culture and changed the context in which leaders and businesses must operate. Do not misunderstand; I wish it had not taken a global pandemic and the loss of millions of precious lives to get the point across. This is a defining moment that has accelerated the need for businesses to constantly seek ways to transform and achieve higher levels of excellence. For so long, the focus in business was all about profits and results. Now, you have plenty of corporations who want and embrace a new set of expectations and requirements for their leaders and employees.

Mark Cuban, the serial entrepreneur and businessman and star of *Shark Tank*, believed that the pandemic could be a defining moment for organizations and their leaders. In a 2020 interview with WBUR Radio's "On Point," he said that leaders and corporations bear responsibility in a crisis such as the Coronavirus pandemic. "If enough companies get it and do better and set a good example of how a company should be run in America 2.0, I think that's how you get momentum."

Ask yourself: *Is the approach that your company is taking gaining momentum? Or are you just doing what you have always done? Have you been awakening to a larger room each day, and embracing all the opportunities that await you?*

Personal mental health challenges and employee well-being concerns became more prevalent than ever in 2020. A global survey found that nearly seven out of ten people are suffering or struggling in their lives. In addition, the U.S. Census Bureau found that a third of Americans show clear signs of clinical depression and anxiety. Even before the COVID-19 pandemic, this was a significant increase.[9]

Hiring managers were then confronted with never-before-seen difficulties in accessing top talent. There has never been a time in history when companies had to balance so many important aspects in how they communicated with their workforce, the resources they offered, and the implications that ensued.

With as much pain as the crisis inflicted on so many organizations all over the world, the room for error becomes exponentially small when you add technological advancements and an ever-growing competitive landscape in almost every sector.

The competitive nature of business will not abate any time soon, while the AI and technology surge will continue to grow with each passing second. Culture is the one thing that all leaders and organizations have at their disposal to build and strengthen their organizational foundation to counteract crises, protect themselves from future threats, and win big.

The Aim of This Book

The aim of this book is to create an actionable playbook that leaders can implement in their day-to-day operations to not only build healthier and better-performing organizations but also drive business impact to heights they never imagined.

My hope is that by the time you finish reading *Culture Is the Way*, you will have a deep and firm understanding of the significance of culture. Hopefully, you will also learn how to drive organizational speed, impact, and excellence while developing your own culture-building framework. Over the years, this framework has had a positive impact and transformed the performance of many leading companies. In this book, some of those examples and their journeys will be shared.

This is not an academic book with complicated theories and hard-to-understand data. I admire and often read many of those books, but this is not one of them. I am determined to take a highly complex subject like organizational culture and distill it down to a relatable approach that will support you in immediately starting to build a great culture for your organization. This book will share real-life examples, stories, and interviews with everyday leaders who have completely transformed the performance of their organizations by becoming passionate culture-builders.

CHAPTER 2

What Exactly Is Culture?

Culture is the deeper level of basic assumptions and beliefs that are shared by members of an organization, that operate unconsciously and define in a basic "taken for granted" fashion an organization's view of itself and its environment.

—Edgar Schein

I am obsessive when it comes to discussing, studying, and building culture.

   As much as I love speaking on stage in front of thousands of people or partnering and working side by side with a senior leadership team to drive cultural excellence, those are not my favorite aspects of my work.

   There is nothing I love more than the pre-work that happens before every speaking engagement and consulting project. Maybe it is the athlete in me that still obsesses over the preparation work that is needed to perform to the best of my ability and make an extraordinary impact, but I truly love that part of the process. And I believe this is an important part of the process when it comes to building an extraordinary culture in a business or organization. *It's the preparation.* A great culture does not emerge by itself. It requires extensive planning, in-depth internal research, mental shifts, collaboration, and more. Starting in Chapter 5, I'll walk you through a five-step process for creating an elite, high-performing culture.

   Every situation, whether it's a 60-minute keynote speech or a year-long journey with a client to create and drive organizational change, needs a unique perspective and implementation strategy.

   Every organization has its own set of challenges and goals, so one of the first things I do is sit down with the senior leadership team and have several lengthy conversations. We delve deeply into where they are now, where they aspire to be, what their current strategy is, and exactly what they expect from me in a partnership role moving forward. It is essential to know how and where I can help.

   Culture is the lifeblood of organizational excellence. The core. The energy. The genetic code. It is front-and-center for leaders who want to improve performance and strategic alignment. It is an organization's heart and soul.

   "Culture is the X-factor," said Noah Rabinowitz, senior partner and global head of Hay Group's Leadership Development Practice. "It's the invisible glue that holds an organization together and ultimately makes the difference between whether an organization is able to succeed in the market or not."

Simply put, it is how well an organization does everything behind closed doors. When you see a high-performing organization that achieves excellence in nearly every aspect of its operations, I will show you a company with an exceptional commitment to fostering and enhancing its culture. The deep-seated purpose of an organization, what it does daily, and the level of impact it has both internally and externally are all aspects of its culture.

Regardless of what a leader says their organizational culture is, the deciding factor lies in the collective mindsets, repeated efforts and actions, and consistent results experienced both inside and outside the organization.

Organizational culture, in my opinion, is like the human body. In so many ways, the human body is fascinating. Every living human being has a set of predetermined genes and DNA that are specific to them and their existence in this world. We used to believe that the genes we were born with determined our fate. It has now been discovered, thanks to advances in modern research and medicine, that our genes only play a role in how we live and the overall quality of our lives.

The difference now is that we can raise the bar in terms of overall quality and health. David Sinclair, a biologist and Harvard Medical School researcher, has fascinating research that delves deeper into this.[1]

Despite our DNA, we can alter the aging process and even reverse it by consuming nourishing foods, managing stress effectively, prioritizing a weekly fitness routine, and investing in positive and healthy relationships. The human body has approximately 37 trillion cells, with each cell playing an important role in how we age, our psychological state, and, ultimately, how long we live.

We can't see our DNA or the cells that make up the human body, or how we go about our daily lives, so we rarely think about them, but we know they exist. What we care about most is how we look on the beach or whether we like what we see when we look in the mirror. Every part of our lives is affected by how well every cell in our body works, from how well we do at work to how happy we feel to the results of our bloodwork panels at our annual physical.

In some ways, organizational culture is very similar. Visible to the naked eye are the results that a company has achieved in the marketplace. We can look at the profit-and-loss statement. We can easily track monthly sales and even break it down by division to see which division is meeting their targets and which is not. By looking at the stock price, we can see how a company is perceived on Wall Street. Employee engagement surveys can reveal how employees currently feel about working for a specific company. There are literally hundreds of ways to track an organization's performance.

Just as our DNA and the trillions of cells in our bodies are influenced positively or negatively by our daily habits and environment, the same can be said for organizational culture. It is not visible to the naked eye, but it is the one thing that enables everything else in an organization to function.

An organization's culture is its DNA. It is equivalent to what oxygen is to the human body. It is needed for an organization to survive, let alone thrive. We can redirect an organization's performance by changing its culture, just as we can reverse the aging process in the human body. Whether an organization has a world-class culture or a toxic one, its future depends on how much attention and focus it puts on growing its culture.

The thing about culture is this: Whether it was created intentionally or not, every organization has one. I was recently speaking with Cecilia, a front-line employee at an advertising firm. She said that her company lacked a culture, which was the main reason she was debating whether or not to leave her current employer.

"What do you mean?" I asked her. "Can you explain a bit more about why you think this?"

"We don't have a culture," Cecilia said. "There is no structure and employees do whatever they want. Along with my usual daily responsibilities, I am putting out at least five fires a day because colleagues didn't follow directions or simply just don't care." She sighed. "To be honest, Matt, I have never even heard the word *culture* from anyone in the company, even the leaders of the company."

With a smile on my face, I responded, "You just told me your company's culture."

"What?" Cecilia threw me a side glance. I think she thought I was *full of it*, to tell you the truth.

I explained in more detail, "Look, Cecilia, it's not just the companies who constantly communicate to their employees, or those who practice their culture's beliefs in everything the company does. Even low-performing companies that never prioritize culture and have toxic workplaces have a culture. You either have a *culture by default* or a *culture by design* that has been intentionally built with as much rigor as the sales and operational strategy."

"Well, we need to improve our company culture, if that's the case," she said.

"Many do," I agreed.

The current results that an organization is experiencing are a result of its culture. If an organization wants to improve its performance, it must become obsessed with changing its culture with fervor and persistence.

We can't solve problems with the same thinking that created the problems in the first place. How do you achieve your own new level of thinking? How do you achieve this new level of belief and mindset so that you can perform optimally as a leader, particularly when confronted with other challenges? You must change the context in which your thoughts emerge. This context, in human terms, is the "biology."

What is the emotional state from which thought emerges? You change that context—the biological and emotional context— and you can change the quality of the thought and the actual thought itself.

When you gain too much weight, you must change your eating and exercise habits. When you don't get enough sleep, you can fix it by being strict about when you go to bed and when you get up in the morning. You review your food and nutritional intake when you have headaches and low energy, and you may make changes to help you perform better. There is simply no excuse in this day and age because science has provided us with every tool that we need to help us become better and perform better. To put it another way, we want to be healthy and energetic despite our DNA and genes. As leaders, if we don't like where we are or the results that our organization has produced thus far because of the current culture, we have the power to change that.

Confusion Around Culture

It was a humbling experience, and I will never forget one conversation. The company tasked me with collaborating with their internal leaders to expedite the implementation of a cultural transformation. We had a twelve-month strategy in place. I had spoken at one of their leadership conferences in Las Vegas six months prior, so I was already familiar with the company.

There were five senior leaders on this kick-off call with me. Within the first ten minutes of our conversation, Derek, the Vice President of Sales said, "Quite frankly, I don't even know how we got here and why we are having this conversation with you, Matt."

I started to respond, but Derek continued, "Please don't take offense to that, because you knocked your speech out of the park for us in Vegas and I know you will be able to help us in a lot of ways. But our people need to be selling, executing, and doing what they're supposed to be doing—and that's NOT more training, more meetings, and engaging in all this culture talk. Besides, we already changed our core values last year. And now we just need to make those updated core values more visible throughout the offices so our teams can get out there and sell!"

"I understand," I told him. "That's why culture is so important, because it is much more than core values and making posters. You need robust leaders who passionately build culture daily. It's a process. It doesn't happen overnight."

"Well, what do you think culture is, Matt?" He seemed genuine.

"Culture is everything and it's nearly impossible to place too much of an emphasis on it," I explained. "It starts with a company's leaders. You must identify your culture targets and then define what your culture stands for. These targets need to align with the company's strategic direction and they're important to execute. I know that your company understands your 'target' and you value your customers. But leaders need to reflect that, too. They need to act as brand ambassadors for your products but also for the culture that you want to build. You need to show that you're living the values yourself before you can expect others to change their own behavior."

Derek nodded.

"It's also vitally important that your employees are in alignment with how they view your company, and the expectations are extremely clear."

Again, Derek nodded, but his eyes glazed over a little, as if he was bored with the topic already. Even though Derek understood sales and marketing, I knew I would need to spend some time helping him and other executives in his company discover their culture's mindset and strengths. I would need to interview key stakeholders and influential members of the organization as needed, then develop plans accordingly to help them improve in all areas.

"Let me explain a little bit more," I said. "In a service business like yours, it's important to deliver the products and services your customers want and that will also enrich their lives, and your company has done that quite well. Perhaps you don't even realize that you have already developed a strong culture in some ways. It's every company's goal to adapt to meet the demands of particular industry environments. For example, organizational cultures in financial services are more likely to emphasize *safety*. There are complex regulations enacted in response to a financial crisis, and careful work and risk management are more critical than ever before in this industry. In contrast, nonprofits are far more purpose-driven, which can reinforce their commitment to a mission by aligning employee behavior around a common goal."

"You're saying that a culture must support the company's goals and plans of the business?"

"Exactly." I could see that Derek was finally beginning to understand.

Leaders must simultaneously consider cultural styles and key organizational and market conditions if they want their culture to drive performance. Region and industry are among the most germane external factors to keep in mind; critical internal considerations include alignment with strategy, leadership, and organizational design.

Luckily for this company, Derek was not directly in charge of its fate. It was still quite alarming, though, that a senior leader of a very respectable and successful organization felt this way. That he was in doubt about the true nature and meaning of culture. Unfortunately, this leader is not alone in what he believes culture is, what it stands for, and what it is intended to represent in an organizational or team environment.

It is this type of mindset that creates confusion, discord, and struggles among leaders when trying to build an organizational culture that they are not only proud of, but most importantly, that delivers real, tangible results. It is important to first understand what culture is.

Driver of Organizational and Team Excellence

There are exceptional companies, average companies, and below-average companies that are on the verge of going out of business at any moment. The same can be said about the world of sports. In football, for example, there are perennial powerhouses that compete for a championship every year, average teams that occasionally have a great year, and bottom-feeders that are lucky to win one game in a season.

Every player in the National Football League is talented. Talent is extremely important, but it is not the deciding factor in whether a team goes on to create a dynasty and compete for the Super Bowl in three of the last five years. When multiple businesses compete in the same market with a similar level of talent, one is destined to break away from the pack and outperform everyone else.

How can this be?

How can a team in professional sports have some of the best talent in the world and still lose most of their games in a given year?

How is it humanly possible for a company to outperform its rivals over a span of a decade with relatively fewer resources than their competitors?

Could it be their belief systems?

Is it because they are committed to organizational excellence and believe wholeheartedly in what they're doing?

These questions, as well as the examples above, have fascinated me since 2010, and I am not alone. Every year, it seems like there is a new article, documentary, or book about a high-performing company or team that has consistently produced remarkable results that have stunned the world.

The one thing these companies and teams have in common is a world-class culture, not the best talent, the most effective strategy, or even the best facilities or training programs. This culture encourages organizational excellence, a "winner's mentality," and confidence in their ability to do well.

Don't get me wrong. Do they have extremely talented individuals who are superior at their work? Absolutely. Do they have a winning strategy implemented that helps them discover pockets of growth to consistently achieve high levels of success? Certainly. Those things are important and very much needed. As a matter of fact, we will touch on some of those areas throughout the rest of this book, but for now, know this: *That is not the driver of their greatness.* The driver of all organizational and team excellence is the culture that has been built and cultivated, day in and day out.

The irony is that everyone wants to focus on the CEO of the enterprise or the star player on the team when these exceptional organizations and teams achieve incredible success over a long period of time. Even though the leaders and head coach often credit the team's culture as the driver of their success, the media and public continue to focus on the star player or leader as the reason for their enormous success. But any great leader or coach will be quick to tell you that their team's culture sets them apart from the rest.

It reminds me of the old adage, "You have to believe it to achieve it." And this isn't some fluffy New Age nonsense. All it means is that if you believe it with all your heart and soul, you will work day and night to achieve whatever it is you desire. And leaders who cultivate this belief system by creating a team or organizational environment that brings out the best in their teams do everything possible to support this.

Legendary football coach Bill Walsh said it best: "The culture precedes positive results. It doesn't get tacked on as an afterthought on your way to the victory stand. Champions behave like champions before they're champions. They have a winning standard of performance before they are winners."

Negative Misconceptions

Everyone interprets the concept of organizational culture differently. If you asked twenty people what their definition of culture is, you would almost certainly get twenty different answers.

One of the most obvious misconceptions about culture is the context in which it is defined. Consider Derek, the Vice President of Sales, who believed that culture meant creating new core values and then simply making them more visible so that his team could go out and sell, sell, sell.

It is nearly impossible to build a great culture if you believe that it entails gathering the senior leadership team for an offsite retreat to develop new core mandates and then plastering those values throughout sales offices and headquarters. It goes much deeper than that.

Workplace culture reflects the values of company leadership and can shape employee interactions and motivations. Organizational culture greatly impacts the success of a business, which is why it's imperative to devote time and effort to understanding how your workplace environment functions and how to enhance it.

Culture Is Not. . .

Before digging deeper into aspects of what culture truly is, I believe it is necessary to first dispel some of the common misconceptions about what culture is not:

- Culture is not the flexibility to work three days per week.
- Culture is not wearing whatever you want to work, such as pajamas, sneakers, cut-off jeans, sweatshirts, etc.
- Culture is not having the liberty to do whatever you want, not showing up when you're supposed to, and working whenever the mood strikes you.
- Culture is not having a manager who never holds you accountable and/or challenges you.
- Culture is not reciting the company's mission statement at team meetings.
- Culture is not having ping-pong tables and other fun games in the office.
- Culture is not supposed to make everyone happy.
- Culture is not a separate aspect of organizational and business execution.
- Culture in a business aspect is not ethnic or discriminatory in any way.

When the examples above are mistaken for what culture stands for, they can be detrimental. I am not suggesting that perks and the examples shared are bad or should never be included in the workplace, but they do not define culture in its entirety.

Once you've laid a solid foundation for the culture you want to build, it's critical to create an environment where people want to come to work every day. The issue has nothing to do with perks or even attire. The problem arises when leaders believe that culture is defined by how many perks they can offer to make their employees happy or how cute the core values are.

I see it far too often. A leader will reach out in the hopes of completely changing their culture, improving the culture they already have, or helping in a merger that will cause cultural friction.

After a few conversations with leaders and learning more about their efforts leading up to the present moment, it has become abundantly clear to me why they are dissatisfied and why performance has suffered. They haven't had the success or momentum they had hoped for because their definition of culture was severely skewed.

Five Key Elements of a Positive Culture

There are many aspects of culture that can significantly improve performance and outcomes, but I will focus on the five essential elements that a positive culture ensures. These five elements are integral to why culture is so important and cannot be ignored if you want to lead your team and organization to the next level.

1. **Employee energy, excitement, and value:** The amount of energy and excitement that culture can inject into an organization is one of the more powerful forces of culture that is rarely discussed and, frankly, difficult to quantify. Star performers and your most ambitious workers may be motivated to set audacious goals and achieve them, but this is not the case for the majority. Many leaders make the mistake of thinking that talking about dominating the competition, sharing divisional goals, and emphasizing financials will motivate their

workforce. Employees can and will be enthusiastic about leaders and managers who invest the time and effort to build a healthier and better culture by involving them in meetings, planning, and strategy sessions, from the highest level to the lowest. The employees want to know they are valued. When this is communicated and consistently implemented by leaders, the amount of energy and enthusiasm generated can be extraordinary. It does not imply that everything is perfect or will be perfect, but the workforce is receiving the message that their future will be brighter and better. That employees are valuable and included in the decision-making process. That they have value. There is tremendous strength in that.

2. **Alignment and togetherness:** A common source of frustration in many organizations is a lack of alignment or a feeling of togetherness as a team. Each division within an organization operates differently from one another, and before long, internal silos can easily develop. Naturally, if you lead the Sales or Marketing division, your responsibilities and goals will differ from those of the Operations and Finance departments. At the end of the day, however, you are all on the same team, working toward a common objective as a unified organization. This is something that great leaders and teams recognize, and culture is the only factor that drives the execution of organizational alignment. I played defense during my football career. I spent most of my time with other linebackers and defensive players, as opposed to offensive players. However, we were all teammates and knew that to win, we had to work together as a unit. Different responsibilities, but a single team pursuing the same primary goal. Every division within an organization will have its own method for executing and setting priorities, but culture is the key to achieving alignment and getting everyone to move in the same direction.

3. **Clear expectations:** An organization that has a culture by default and has never prioritized defining their culture will eventually face performance and morale issues. The reason for this is that if your culture is never defined, there are no

clear expectations of what is required and expected of every team member to help the organization win. Not having clear expectations is far more detrimental than just poor performance alone. Some 43% of employees believe that their job description is clear. That is less than half of employees who go to work each day without a clear understanding of what is important and what they should be doing. Even worse, only 41% of employees agree that their job descriptions accurately reflect the daily work they perform. Employees who do not have clear expectations at work experience more stress, anxiety, and loneliness.[2]

Having a defined and positive workplace culture aids in mitigating and preventing these costly issues. In great and healthy cultures, there is clarity on the company's core purpose and priorities, and employees receive consistent feedback.

4. **Accelerate execution:** Culture drives and accelerates how well an organization's operational and business strategy is executed. Over the years, I've spoken with far too many leaders who believed that culture was separate from their strategy. Your strategy does not carry out the strategy on its own. That is the job and sole responsibility of the culture you build and manage. Strategy is critical to winning, but don't overlook culture in developing your strategy. They collaborate concurrently to speed up execution and enhance impact. Healthy and strong cultures help to instill and promote the daily behaviors needed to win and execute the strategy.

5. **Talent attraction and development:** A potent and crucial aspect of culture is the role it plays in attracting top talent and developing existing talent. When you create a great culture that brings out the best in everyone, challenges others positively, and consistently drives winning behaviors in the marketplace, word spreads quickly. Everyone wants to work for a company that makes them feel like they are a part of something special and that they can contribute to the overall mission. The right culture is also important in creating an

environment that safely pushes others out of their comfort zone to try new things and broaden their mindset. There is a reason why the best football teams and world-class enterprises not only attract the best talent, but also have a track record of molding and developing the talent they already have, which adds to the bottom line exponentially.

CHAPTER 3

The Dilemma Traps

Your big picture will never be a masterpiece if you ignore the tiny brush strokes.

—Andy Andrews

I should have been in bed, sleeping, like everyone else.

On a gloomy, rainy Saturday morning in April 2020, I received a phone call from Peter, a senior leader of a company that I had been working with for some years. I normally don't receive too many work-related calls on Saturday morning, so I was almost certain that there was an emergency that needed immediate attention.

When I answered the phone and said hello, Peter, breathless, quickly shouted, "I can't believe I waited this long to start prioritizing our culture and working just as hard on it as much as we spend on growing the business."

I tried to quickly interrupt his self-sabotaging tangent, but he went on to tell me, "I am scattered. They are scattered. Everything is just scattered! Our entire workforce is working remote now and the impact on our business is looking to be much worse than I originally thought."

The tone of this leader's voice conveyed his excruciating pain. We were only a month into the global pandemic, and none of us could have predicted what would happen. To be honest, I recall having many conversations with at least a dozen different leaders who downplayed the gravity of what was to come.

I assumed that this conversation with Peter would breeze right over, and we would get back to business as usual. I tried to calm the senior leader down that Saturday morning. "Look, Peter, you're accurate in your assessment that you should have prioritized culture years ago, but remember, the next best time to do this is now."

Peter was not alone in wishing he had paid greater attention to culture.

I grabbed a cup of coffee and then spent the next hour strategizing with him on how to revitalize the company's culture, generate enthusiasm, instill passion in him and his team, and move forward. Peter was one of those who was always analyzing trends and graphs, which generally lose all focus on culture.

After drinking a pot of coffee, Peter settled down. "Thanks, Matt, for taking time to talk. And I apologize for disturbing you on a Saturday morning."

"Hey, no problem," I said. "I'm glad to help."

I have had many heartfelt conversations with leaders over the past three years, and if we all had known the complications that the pandemic was going to create, I bet every one of them would have changed their approach in the blink of an eye.

Similar to my meeting with Peter, a consistent theme has surfaced in nearly all my conversations with senior leaders and managers over the past three years. The common thread is that almost every leader voiced remorse for putting culture on the backburner for something they thought was more essential.

We shouldn't wait for a crisis or global pandemic to prioritize culture and make it an integral part of every function within the organization. For many reasons, the last three years have been extremely difficult. In retrospect, the first half of 2020 was a blur. Hazy. Distorted. Isolated.

Even now, I find it difficult to believe that the entire world was shut down at one point. Not only did leaders and organizations around the world have to scramble to keep their operations running, but they also had to balance the ongoing health implications of their workforce. Moreover, for a period of time, all communication with employees and coworkers was conducted exclusively via Zoom, Skype, and other online video platforms. The world was in disarray, and the uncertainty of the future was astronomical.

When it comes to leaders at every level within an organization, one of the more subtle but extremely dangerous traps to fall into is believing that there are more important imperatives to be paying attention to other than culture. For a lot of leaders, it wasn't until a global pandemic completely shifted and revolutionized the vital role that culture plays in how an organization performs in turbulent times, but also how healthy that organization truly is at its core.

I am sure you have either seen first-hand or heard of examples of companies who never panicked and still performed exceptionally well. On the other hand, there are countless stories and unfortunate examples of organizations that completely collapsed when the crisis hit, which prevented them from capitalizing on the incredible opportunities that all crises present. This begs the question: *How can we future-proof our organizations as leaders and stay focused on what matters most?*

We need to be aware of the shiny object syndrome.

The Shiny Object Syndrome

The culture dilemma that sabotages most culture-building efforts is convincing leaders that there is something more significant and vital that they should be paying attention to instead of culture. There are many shiny objects that present themselves in every organization, and leaders are quick to believe that attacking or embracing that next shiny object with decisive action is the surest path to growth. They often overlook the very simple things that can propel them to success.

Shiny objects consist of more than just action items and operating procedures. Certain mindsets and beliefs can also take the form of shiny objects. Depending on the organization and industry, the "shiny objects" will look different. Here are a few examples to help you understand what I mean:

- The brand new and exhilarating technology system that was recently installed which is supposedly going to increase the productivity of the salesforce by 25%.

- A new HR tracking system which will help the effectiveness of one's ability to promote top talent and enhance the efficiency of the current candidate pool.

- A detailed and running list of one hundred initiatives leaders must complete by the end of the year in response to the employee survey results that came back a month ago.

- Plan and attend an offsite leadership retreat to develop and refine the company's strategy for the year ahead.

- Rigorously track sales and revenue numbers every month and do whatever it takes to hit the numbers.

- Resting on laurels and continuing to do the same thing over and over when things are going great, thinking that the same result will continue to repeat itself.
- Everything is fine when we are profitable.

These examples illustrate how simple it is to fall prey to the "shiny object syndrome." Just like my client, Peter. Long before we started working together, Peter expressed his desire to build a great culture for his people, but he was frequently defeated or distracted by the numerous shiny objects. He had been so preoccupied with pursuing all the enticing opportunities that he had overlooked the one thing that would have accelerated all his efforts. The creation and ongoing development of a strong organizational culture.

I could give you many more examples of shiny objects, but hopefully you get the idea. I am not implying that these matters are unimportant. Some of the listed examples are essential for constructing a successful and high-performing organization. However, the problem with many of these shiny objects is that they cause leaders to become blind. They are quick to jump from one shiny object to the next, believing that it will fill the void left by ignoring where they should really be spending their time: developing and growing their culture.

The paradox of the shiny object syndrome is that culture is the fundamental building block that enables an organization to execute and succeed at virtually everything else, including many of the examples of shiny objects listed earlier. When an organization lacks the right culture, which ultimately serves as the foundation of excellence for how well it performs, there will be a collapse in performance, and eventually profit and growth.

Culture Is Not Sexy

I can already hear you asking, "Matt, if culture is really as important as you say it is, then why wouldn't every leader obsess over it and more organizations strive to have a world-class culture?"

This is by far the most popular question that I receive. Whether it be via an email, after a speaking engagement when I come off-stage, or during coaching sessions with consulting clients of mine, in some way, shape, or form this question is presented to me.

The answer is easy, though. The reason why culture is often neglected is because there is nothing sexy about it.

You know what's appealing and incredibly sexy?

Aggressively tracking sales on a monthly or weekly basis while being able to visually see if those numbers are climbing upwards or falling downwards. Or undergoing a digital transformation meant to streamline the selling process, something that has all the bells and whistles that will hopefully boost operational efficiency.

Now, those are appealing and sexy.

When most leaders and people managers hear the word "culture," they rarely drop everything else they're working on to focus solely on culture because it's so appealing. In fact, it's usually the exact opposite.

I'm not going to sugarcoat the truth and promise that there will be no bumps in the road. Building a great organizational culture that drives business impact is excruciatingly difficult, and staying consistent with it is even more difficult. It becomes some of the most important work that leaders will ever do in their careers.

I've discovered and continue to live by a life-changing motto that can be directly applied to culture:

If something is hard and the more likely I am to resist it, the more it is usually going to benefit my life and the harder I should attack it.

This motto applies directly to culture. You or other leaders you work with are likely to resist it and even question why precious time and energy are being spent on something with few immediate benefits. However, the fact that you are opposed to the idea in the first place tells you everything you need to know.

"The more important an activity is to your soul's evolution, the more resistance you will feel to it—the more fear you will feel," said Steven Pressfield, best-selling author of one of my favorite books, *The War of Art*.[1] This quote encapsulates it perfectly and explains why so many leaders resist and put culture to the side. Because culture is so important to the evolution of an organization, fear, neglect, and resistance become entrenched.

In my experience working with leadership teams, when there is a consensus on an idea within an organization and every leader is in complete agreement, there is a good chance that the idea is not currently the highest priority. Because it's far too simple. Don't get me wrong. I am a big believer in leaders achieving quick wins and gaining momentum.

Does this mean for every decision where the leadership team is in complete agreement that they should not move forward?

Of course not, but I believe it is essential for leadership teams to develop a weekly team meeting where they can come together and spend adequate time discussing what they should or should not act on.

Typically, what is needed to take an organization to the next level is extremely difficult and pushes each leader beyond his or her comfort zone, so everyone will initially resist it. It will challenge almost everyone while putting to the test their long-held, stagnant belief systems.

Of course, this analogy applies to all aspects of life. Smokers who want to quit are often aware of the steps required to break the bad habit. But when you take the time to consider those steps and the pain you will most likely experience, you will dread what lies ahead because you know it will be incredibly challenging. After a long and stressful day, you might find it appealing to grab a cigarette. This is the only thing you have known during your decade-long smoking habit. However, it will not bring you any closer to kicking the unhealthy habit.

If you want to lose weight and become a healthier version of yourself, changing your eating habits is much more difficult than it sounds. Many of us use food as an emotional outlet when times are tough, and even thinking about giving up some of your favorite foods can be overwhelming, to say the least.

These are some of the reasons why smokers struggle to quit, and why people who want to lose weight revert to the unhealthy habits they vowed to abandon once and for all. To some extent, all these people were victims of the "shiny object syndrome."

The same is true for leaders who put in the effort to create an extraordinary and impactful organizational culture. It's not enticing or sexy. What makes it even more challenging is that at least a dozen shiny objects will hang deflectors on your perception of culture throughout the year, distracting you from where you should direct your attention.

Boeing: An American Giant That Lost Its Way

What is at stake when an organization's leaders cave in and succumb to the shiny object syndrome? In short, everything could be on the line. I recently watched the Netflix documentary *Downfall: The Case Against Boeing*, directed by Rory Kennedy and produced by Brian Grazer and Ron Howard.

The documentary does an excellent job of highlighting how Boeing executives were driven by greed and only cared about increasing profits, resulting in two horrific plane crashes in 2018 and 2019. In and of itself, the fact that hundreds of lives were lost is incredibly tragic. But what makes this example even more tragic is the fact that Boeing executives at the time were aware of the malfunction responsible for both crashes and chose to do nothing about it.

Boeing was once an American business giant known for its safety procedures and fantastic culture in which employees thoroughly enjoyed working. The leaders at Boeing were swayed by the shiny object syndrome, which in this case was greed and adopting a profit-first mentality over everything else.

When Boeing became aware of the malfunction, which prompted many of their mechanical engineers to raise their voices and speak out about it, executives were adamant about keeping the information from leaking. If the problem had become public, it would have hampered their desire to get the upgraded 737 Max into the market, jeopardizing profits.

It's one thing to move with ferocious speed and have audacious goals, as every great company embodies these traits in some way, but it must never come at the expense of your culture. Or human lives. It might even pay off temporarily, or you might think it will until a tragedy happens because you didn't use good judgment, like what happened to Boeing.

The decision to take the easy way out and avoid building and preserving your culture at all costs will always catch up with you in the end. When you're driving one of the greatest companies in America at the time, it's easy to let greed take over and only think in terms of profit. It's easy to keep doing what you've always done, especially if you've had a lot of success in business for the last twenty years.

However, as I noted previously, just because something is simple or presents little opposition does not mean that it should be the focus of your energy and attention.

The Boeing example may be an extreme example of what is at stake for us as leaders when we become too attached and distracted by the shiny object syndrome, but the moral of the story is usually the same, regardless of the example. It would have been incredibly difficult for Boeing executives to address the problem head-on because it would not only have slowed their original route to market plans, but it would have cost them financially. In some ways, Boeing may be seen as a company that prioritized greed over safety, and in some ways, that would be true.

But even so, I see it as a company's leaders succumbing to the culture dilemma. They had to choose between two undesirable choices. The first option was to continue doing what they had always done, which was to pride themselves on being world-class in building safe and highly functional airplanes while never cutting corners. If they had chosen this path, it would have slowed them down and likely caused a temporary decline in earnings.

Or should they allow monetary gain to influence their decision-making, even if it means acting unethically and endangering the lives of other people?

Unfortunately, the executives at Boeing chose the latter.

However, bad decisions made by others can be used as a teaching tool if we not only learn from them but also apply and practice what we have learned.

The Great Turnaround

For every example of an organization that lost its way and neglected to put effort into culture-building, there are just as many examples of companies that did the exact opposite. In 2006, the famous automaker Ford Motor Company was having a hard time. This is thought to be one of the most impressive turnarounds in American business history.

The company was losing billions of dollars, and the future of a once-iconic American corporation was in grave danger. Alan Mulally was a senior executive at Boeing at the time, and he was responsible for not only turning the company around after the terrorist attacks of September 11, 2001, but also catapulting the company back to absolute dominance.

When Ford needed a new CEO to take over the company and dig them out of the hole they found themselves in, no one was more desired than Boeing's Alan Mulally. Mulally eventually accepted the job, and the rest is history. So much has been written about the astounding turnaround that Mulally engineered while he was at Ford, but for the purposes of this book, it is not the turnaround I wish to highlight, no matter how impressive it was. It was how Mulally did it and where he chose to focus his time and energy.

Alan Mulally attributes Ford's turnaround to an obsessive focus on putting people first, working together as "One Ford Team," and having a compelling vision of the future.

The common thread among all struggling companies is that while there may be some operational and strategic issues that need to be addressed, the main reason for the steep decline is usually culture-related. Alan Mulally dedicated everything he had to building Ford's future with the people at Ford and changing the Ford culture by making it the primary focus from day one.

Even though some very beneficial strategic decisions were made, it wasn't solely the company's strategy. It did not involve being influenced by the opinions of the general public about what Ford should do.

When culture serves as the foundation and people come first, incredible forces rush to your aid, allowing you to see things more clearly and eventually become even greater than before.

How to Avoid the Culture Dilemma Traps

These were two examples from two different companies, each with a radically different outcome. In life and in business, where we are now and where we will go in the future are directly related to the daily choices that we make.

The number of decisions a leader must make every minute of every day can be overwhelming at times, particularly for those who are new to management. But the good news is that when we are aware of the choices we make and how each choice affects someone or something else, we are in a much better position to improve our decision-making ability.

When our decision-making ability as a leader improves, so do the outcomes and experiences created for employees, the organization, and customers.

The first step in overcoming the "shiny object syndrome" is realizing that it attacks from all directions. However, awareness is only half the battle. Let's look at some ways we can take it a step further so that culture-building efforts don't get sabotaged and lose their intended impact.

1. **Don't underestimate culture.** This may appear too simple and obvious, but most attempts to build, change, or improve culture fall short because leaders underestimate culture from the start. Your culture will suffer as a result if you believe that culture is just a word or that there are twenty other more important imperatives.

2. **For everything you add, be willing to subtract something.** I am continually astounded by the fact that some leadership teams intend to pursue ninety initiatives or strategic objectives in a single calendar year. No wonder they ask each other at the end of the year why a large percentage of initiatives failed miserably or never even got off the ground. The dilemma trap and "shiny object syndrome" constantly throw grand ideas in front of you, so you are quick to jump to the next cool project and completely lose focus on culture. It is only a matter of time before leadership teams become overburdened and performance suffers as a result. For each addition you make, whether it is a new meeting on the calendar, a new policy, or an initiative, consider what you can eliminate.

3. **Be ruthlessly clear about your priorities.** When it comes to leaders who fall into the dilemma trap, I have noticed a common theme over the years. They are exceptionally intelligent individuals, but below-average decision-makers due to a lack of organizational clarity regarding their priorities. A half-hearted attempt to spend one day with your leadership team mapping out the strategy and a few vague goals for the year will not be enough. Be ruthlessly clear about who you are as an organization, where you want to go, and the action plan for achieving those goals.

CHAPTER 4

The Five Roadblocks to Cultural Excellence

If the rate of change on the outside exceeds the rate of change on the inside, the end is near.

—Jack Welch

"If it ain't broke, don't fix it," I've heard people say that my entire life.

To be honest, I've never understood this. I've always been the type of person who is looking for the next big thing. The upgraded version. The best of the best. And who wouldn't want that?

Sure, if a friend or family member already has something they think is great, why would they go through the trouble of buying a new one if what they have is adequate? Perhaps they have a good enough refrigerator that they've been using for the past twenty years. They might say, "Why in the world would I want a new fridge when this old one works just fine?"

For starters, older refrigerators consume more electricity than newer models. Simply ask a salesperson at any appliance store. That's because when a refrigerator stops working, it consumes more electricity as it struggles to keep a cool temperature despite a faulty compressor, a worn-out motor, and leaking seals. Refrigerators have become much more sophisticated and energy-efficient over the last twenty years. According to the American Council for an Energy-Efficient Economy, and the National Resources Defense Council, despite new features such as defrost and ice-making, a new typical refrigerator uses only 25% as much electricity as one sold in the 1970s.

Families who replace their old refrigerators notice immediate savings on their energy bills. And yet, some might continue to say, "If it ain't broke, don't fix it."

The point is that people are resistant to change. Even if it's as simple as switching to a new refrigerator that will end up saving them money while also providing new sleek and convenient features, they still find it difficult.

Consider this in terms of business. Simply because a certain structure and method of doing things have worked in your organization for twenty years does not guarantee that those same strategies will continue to work in 2023 and beyond. Why? Because we live in a constantly evolving and progressing world.

Most business leaders today are familiar with the Blockbuster Video story. It was legendary, having been founded in 1985 and having been one of the most iconic brands in the video rental space. People enjoyed walking into a Blockbuster store on any given day of the week and perusing the aisles for a video they could rent for several days. Blockbuster had 84,300 employees worldwide and 9,094 stores at its peak back in 2004.

So, what happened?

Where are all the Blockbuster Video stores nowadays?

Netflix approached Blockbuster in 2000 and asked if they wanted to purchase Netflix for $50 million. The Blockbuster CEO was not interested in the offer because he considered Netflix to be a "very small niche business" in comparison to the behemoth Blockbuster. The latest news was that Netflix, whose system allowed members to rent videos that were mailed to them (which the members would watch and then return in the mail when finished), was losing money at the time.

Blockbuster must have believed that their business model was superior to that of the budding Netflix company. It's possible their motto was "If it ain't broke, don't fix it."

Instead of purchasing Netflix or changing their business models and developing new programs to include online streaming services or sending videos through the postal system, Blockbuster continued to do what they had always done. Purchases and rentals were made available in-store. As a result, they had grown accustomed to the status quo and did not see the need for change or to embrace growth.

Unable to transition toward a digital, streaming model, Blockbuster eventually was forced to file for bankruptcy in 2010.

Netflix built a $25 billion annual revenue stream from its subscribers in just 12 years, and as of 2022, Netflix had nearly 220 million subscribers worldwide.[1] There was a 27.22% increase in 2021 over 2020 in its annual gross profit of $12.365 billion, and a 24.96% increase in 2020 over 2019 in its annual gross profit of $9.72 billion.[2]

Netflix recognized the need for constant growth, and instead of taking the "If it ain't broke, don't fix it" attitude, they have continued to improve their services by expanding their offerings to include climate change specials, docuseries, talks by bestselling authors, and commentaries from political and sports figures. Netflix has continuously adapted and modified its platform to expand beyond its original offerings.

Blockbuster, on the other hand, like so many other companies, was afraid to change their old ways of doing things and merely try something new. When you hear the Netflix-Blockbuster example, you might think it was more of an innovation or complacency issue with Blockbuster than a culture failure. But I respectfully disagree. Culture serves as the internal compass for an organization's fundamental beliefs, how the organization behaves daily, and its level of market performance. Their culture at the time was not supporting them in cultivating and demanding the winning behaviors required to adapt and prevail. A lack of innovation and ineffective leadership were unintended consequences of their existing organizational culture.

What would have happened if Blockbuster had had a culture that discouraged complacency at all costs while constantly imagining possible roadblocks and reinventing themselves as a result? We can only imagine.

On the other hand, despite their current success, Netflix never seems to allow complacency to take over and drive their decision-making process; instead they envision the roadblocks that they could face in the future. For example, Netflix CEO Reed Hastings often has his staff imagine Netflix is on the verge of failure ten years from now. The leadership team starts making a list and having productive discussions about everything that could potentially destroy them. Even at the pinnacle of success, they consider what could go wrong and what the organization's leaders should be thinking about.[3]

This is visionary, leadership thinking at its best.

I believe we would be having a very different conversation if Blockbuster had been envisioning future roadblocks and discussing solutions at the height of its success. It's no surprise that one of these businesses went extinct, while the other one has thrived.

This begs the questions:

1. Why is it so difficult to change, even when we know it's necessary for our future?
2. Why do most change and transformation efforts never gain the momentum that leaders desire?

People, in general, are afraid of change and the unknown that it brings, and they resist it. However, if your company does not change, it will remain stagnant, indicating that it will never reach its full potential. Even though many people may think they don't like change, I believe that change in and of itself is not the problem. The real issue is the fear. The fear of letting go of old behaviors and ways of doing things, especially when things seem to be going relatively well in the present.

Almost every business leader today will agree on the importance of building a company that is constantly learning and evolving. But even organizations renowned for their learning and development efforts often find it challenging to remain consistent. Take Toyota, for example. The company had to recall nearly 9 million vehicles nearly a decade ago. A key pillar of their foundational strategy is continuous improvement, and the company's leaders said that their failures were in large part a result of them straying from that pillar.[4]

Outside of initiating change and looking for ways to improve even when things are going well, most organizations and their leaders fail to remain consistent and committed to the process.

At this very moment, there are probably a lot of companies trying to change, improve, and build a better culture. They will embark on a cultural change journey in the coming months or are currently in the process. However, it is very likely that these same companies not only will fall short of their goal of developing a better and higher-performing culture but will also revert to the old way of doing things that they so desperately wanted to change in the first place.

If it came down to pure effort and determination, most organizations would be able to muscle their way across the finish line and successfully get the job done. There is a reason why most change and transformation efforts fail, and sometimes never even reach the halfway point. According to Harvard Business School professor John Kotter's research, nearly 70% of organizational change efforts fall short of the desired goal.[5]

The New Economic Order of Changing Culture

Our world is literally in Zoom-mode. Fast-paced. Stress-driven. Days go by in a blur.

Can't fly out to the next business meeting? No problem.

Tick-tock. Time is wasting. We'll just Zoom-meet.

Things are changing so fast every day that we can barely keep up. New business systems, new AI products to help us improve productivity, new technology to help us process the data that's emerging from all corners of the world. Honestly, it's as if our world has created what amounts to a *New Economic Order of Changing Culture*, and those companies that continually reinvent themselves to adapt to the ongoing changing times and to keep pace with our evolving habits and work methods are more likely to survive than those who don't.

As a leader, changing or upgrading your culture or going through any organizational change, for that matter, can seem like a daunting task. For the leaders and organizations that are successfully able to accomplish such a feat, we often sit back with deep admiration and think to ourselves, "I wish we could do that."

The truth is that you and your organization *can* do that, and you *can* accomplish more than you ever imagined. It's not just a matter of knowing how to successfully drive and execute culture change, which we will cover in the coming chapters, but also of knowing how to anticipate and overcome the common roadblocks to those changes.

When an organization is getting ready to change its culture, improve certain areas of its existing culture, or go through a complete transformation, the potential roadblocks and challenges on the journey ahead are often overlooked or ignored.

A lot of time and effort should not be spent worrying about what might go wrong or worrying about the possibility of failing, as this can prevent the kind of innovation and boldness needed to succeed. However, I've seen a number of culture change and transformation efforts fall apart because leaders were unprepared when they were confronted with numerous setbacks and were unable to adapt and keep moving forward. They were unprepared for the roadblocks, pitfalls, and obstacles they would eventually run into.

If you want to continuously improve your company's culture, you must recognize that you will always face obstacles and difficulties along the way. Every organization and leader will face a distinct set of obstacles that can range from small stepping-stones to massive boulders. What matters most is how prepared you and your company will be to respond to and overcome those roadblocks.

Depending on the current state or size of your organization, as well as the industry it operates in, the challenges will vary from company to company. However, there are a handful of persistent roadblocks that prevent organizations from achieving cultural excellence.

The following are five roadblocks I've encountered while working with a diverse group of leadership teams and organizations over the years. We were able to build and achieve cultural excellence over time because we became aware of these roadblocks from the very beginning.

My primary goal has always been to interact directly with managers and leaders at all levels on the front lines. I did not want to rely solely on statistical data and research but rather on first-hand accounts of the challenges faced by those responsible for fostering a culture that exemplifies speed, impact, and excellence. As a result, over the last few years, I've worked with over 150 senior leaders and managers from a wide range of organizations across multiple industries. We identified hundreds of roadblocks and challenges during our meetings, but the five listed below were constants in nearly every conversation.

The Five Roadblocks to Cultural Excellence

1. Lukewarm Leadership Buy-In

2. All Slogans and No Action

3. Temptation of Instant Gratification

4. Distortion and Distraction

5. Lack of Cascading Change

It's important to remember that even if you're aware of these five potential roadblocks and have a strategy in place to overcome them, success is not a given. The pursuit of perfection is a futile endeavor, and it should not even be a target. Because if an organization isn't being tested and knocked down on a regular basis, chances are it isn't experimenting or moving with great urgency. Similarly, in life, if we open our hearts and minds to expansion and learning from every experience, the failures can hold tremendous value. Turning failures into successes is a trait found in all great leaders.

Let's take a closer look at each of the five roadblocks that frequently debilitate many leaders and organizations in their pursuit of cultural excellence, as well as ideas to help you overcome them.

Roadblock #1: Lukewarm Leadership Buy-In

Not all aspects of world-class culture-building consist of a top-down approach, as you will learn more about in this book, but lukewarm leadership buy-in is without a doubt the greatest roadblock of them all. Especially in the beginning stages of building culture when driving excitement and momentum is an absolute imperative.

Deloitte conducted a leadership study and discovered that the quality of senior leaders had a significant impact on analyst viewpoints about whether companies would succeed.

The findings revealed that companies with perceived effective leadership received a 15% equity premium on average, while companies with perceived ineffective leadership received a 19% discount. These findings support an adage that leaders make or break organizations daily. At the intersection of effective leadership and a strong culture, an organization can achieve dominance in the marketplace.[6]

Unfortunately, I would say that this is not only one of the greater challenges that an organization faces, but also one of the most common roadblocks that occurs. There will be many reasons for lukewarm leadership buy-in. Whether an organization currently has a relatively healthy or toxic workplace environment, there will generally be some pushback.

Most senior leadership teams consist of accomplished leaders with a wealth of experience, and the last thing the majority of them will want to do is shift their leadership style or change how they have done things for the past ten to twenty years. This mentality is a huge barrier in the initial stages of building culture, but quite frankly, also in the execution of all other organizational change efforts. The message that is sent to the entire organization comes directly from the leaders of an organization. No matter how minuscule or important a matter may seem, everything that is verbally communicated, how it is communicated, daily actions that are taken, and even body language of a leader can send shockwaves across an organization. Many leaders have great intentions, but wildly underestimate their level of influence and how often others look to them on how to think and behave in any given situation.

The best and most effective leaders fully understand that it is their duty and responsibility not only to lead the way, but also to serve as a role model for the desired behaviors that they want to instill throughout an organization.

Let's use the example of Southern Glazer's Wine and Spirits of Illinois (SGWS-IL) to highlight the importance of a strong commitment from the senior leadership team. When I first started working with them in 2018 to help build their culture and maximize the performance of the leadership team, there was a varying degree of commitment and "buy-in" from the senior leadership team. There were those who were completely "all-in" while others were wondering, "Why in the world are we having monthly and quarterly meetings added to the calendar for multiple hours at a time?"

"After all," they argued, "We're already a high-performing organization experiencing great success in the marketplace."

One of those leaders who was fully onboard from the very beginning was a gentleman named Mike Housey. Mike serves as the Vice President and General Sales Manager of Southern Glazer's Wine and Spirits of Illinois (SGWS-IL). He is what I would deem as a rare commodity as a leader. He is a total culture fanatic and has been vying for a more intensive focus on building a better culture for years. Their culture wasn't bad by any stretch of the means, but there were certainly key areas of improvement, mainly starting with the senior leaders and all people managers within the company. Even with Mike's passion and devotion to build a better culture for the organization, that wasn't the initial reaction from other key senior leaders.

There were two other senior leaders who were ultimately going to determine the success and the overall impact of the culture. These two were not only very influential within the organization and exceptionally talented, but they were also some of the brightest leaders that I have had the good fortune of working with.

The challenge was that a few key leaders were wondering if there was really a need for a new approach, given their combined experience and the successful results they were already delivering. Did they need to make an even bigger impact? Was it necessary?

The task of altering the behavior of accomplished leaders with a wealth of experience was not an easy one, and it stays a constant challenge for most organizations. Most people simply do not want to tell their superstar performers to change.

Terry Brick and Michael Thompson are the two leaders I'm referring to. Terry Brick is arguably one of the most exceptional leaders I've ever met. He is SGWS-IL's Executive Vice President and General Manager. His ability to consistently perform under extreme pressure and connect with others in order to make them feel special is remarkable. Terry is well known in the wine and spirits industry, and for good reason.

Michael Thompson was the Senior Vice President of Commercial Strategy and Planning at the time. He was most often the smartest person in the room, with an unyielding desire not only to be the best, but also to demand the best from everyone else. Terry and Mike were somewhat engaged and actively taking part in all of our leadership development and culture work, but they were not complete "buy-ins" in the way we needed. They were more lukewarm in the beginning.

If Mike Housey and I could impact and change Terry and Mike's perspectives on culture, that would cascade across the company to the twenty other senior leaders to a degree, and if not *completely*, at least send a strong message to the rest of the organization.

Before Mike Housey and I even started creating the culture roadmap journey, the first couple of months were obsessively focused on bringing the top team together and driving a strong connection as to why culture needed to be the foundation of everything else moving forward.

Not only did that level of focus and prioritization on positively shaping the leadership team from the beginning serve as a key ingredient in SGWS-IL achieving remarkable results over the years, but Terry Brick and Michael Thompson are now huge culture advocates.

As the leader of SGWS-IL, it wasn't until Terry Brick went from being a lukewarm buy-in to becoming fully immersed in the process of shaping the organization's culture that things really started to gain momentum.

Roadblock #2: All Slogans and No Action

The second roadblock that can prevent an organization from achieving cultural excellence and cause a great number of headaches is when culture is viewed as nothing more than some meaningless slogans.

As I shared in previous chapters, if you believe that building a great culture comes down to hanging posters with your mottos and core values written on them throughout the office or simply including more perks, you run the risk of promoting fluff that lacks real substance.

I recently had an intriguing conversation with Jonathan, who is a middle-level manager at a technology firm. Jonathan has been with the company for ten years and has seen quite a few changes in leadership during his tenure at the firm.

One day Jonathan and I were sitting in the break-room talking over a cup of coffee. He said, "Matt, it seems like the change in leadership over the years has really hurt the company's ability to make sufficient progress in building a great culture."

"What do you mean?" I asked him. "Do you think there are problems with your company's leadership?"

I knew that even though high turnover rates and major changes in leadership roles can negatively hurt not only the performance but also the culture of an organization, I sensed there was more to the problem than just that.

"It's hard to put into words," Jonathan said.

"Can you dig a little deeper into what the real challenges have been in your company?" I knew that leaders had to dig deep to uncover the real, core issues.

"I guess the real issue has been that words and affirmations are how we have always attempted to build culture here." Jonathan shrugged his shoulders. "Kind of like that Nike motto: *Just do it*. I mean, what does that really mean if you think about it? It sounds good, and it's a great slogan to put on coffee mugs and t-shirts, but does it really change a company's culture?"

I smiled. "Yeah, I know what you mean. There are hundreds of slogans like that on posters everywhere in offices across the country. And they're nice, sure, but those slogans don't build or *change* culture."

Words don't build culture or change culture by themselves. It takes action.

True cultural change starts when behavioral change at scale begins to take root. And not just changing behaviors from time to time or for a few months at a time. It must be a long-term process with repeated changes in behavior that create a new cultural paradigm and become the new norm.

I have seen leaders confuse "most of the time" behaviors with "repeatable" behaviors. The difference between the two is what separates the organizations that win some of the time compared to those that win all of the time. Doing something most of the time, especially in the context of exchanging a negative behavior for a new and more positive behavior, is a good first step in the right direction, but it's still just a step. Doing something *repeatedly*, to the point where it becomes ingrained into what an organization does daily and becomes common practice, is where cultural excellence lies.

Culture is not just about turning values into behaviors. It's about turning values into *repeatable* behaviors, into actions that become daily habits that are shared across the organization. The conversation with Jonathan served as a real-life example of how, when earlier attempts to change cultures have failed, we are quick to blame turnover, market conditions, stiff competition, and ever-increasing demands. There is no doubt that these things do lead to frustration and prevent cultural excellence to an extent, but most of the time it all comes back to a lack of behavioral shifts that are needed to create the new cultural paradigm.

Measuring the separation gap is a very practical way to think about this. The separation gap is made up of what an organization says is important to them, what they do daily, and how it is interpreted by internal and external stakeholders (Figure 4.1). This can be very beneficial because, if you ask most leaders and managers if they are living their values, the answer will usually be a resounding yes. When you're too invested in your current role and going a million miles per hour, it's exceptionally difficult to take a step back and take inventory. Even when the internality is in the right place, if there is a large gap between what is said and what is done, chances are it will come across as all slogans and no action.

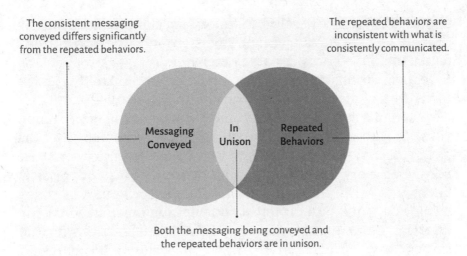

The consistent messaging conveyed differs significantly from the repeated behaviors.

The repeated behaviors are inconsistent with what is consistently communicated.

Messaging Conveyed

In Unison

Repeated Behaviors

Both the messaging being conveyed and the repeated behaviors are in unison.

FIGURE 4.1   The Separation Gap

Roadblock #3: The Temptation of Instant Gratification

Nothing satisfies us as humans more than instant gratification. Before we do or commit to anything, we often ask ourselves or others how long it will take to reap the benefits or experience the results. Our world is dominated by instant gratification, and many businesses have grown significantly wealthy by promoting and selling a false narrative centered on achieving immediate results.

If you turn on the television, you will almost certainly see a commercial for a specific dietary pill that claims to help you lose fifty pounds in thirty days. If you open your favorite social media app, there's a good chance you'll come across an influencer who is fervently promoting the idea that you can look a certain way if you just follow a special diet for fifteen days. What about the online course that promises to make you wealthy if you invest a specific amount of money in bitcoin and watch your financial freedom blossom before your eyes in just sixty days? What about the reality TV star's Instagram account, which posts lavish photos of expensive jewelry and cars while claiming that you can have that life too if you join their mastermind group? And don't forget about the newly released eBook that is being promoted on Facebook, promising that you can build a successful business in thirty days while only working one hour per week.

The sad thing about these pipedream claims is not the individual or company promoting and profiting from them, but the fact that people all over the world cave in and buy into these false narratives every day. Why? Because the lure of instant gratification is a powerful emotion and a force that draws them in. When it comes to building a powerful and winning organizational culture, the temptation of instant gratification lurks around every corner, ready to derail you. Almost all leaders and managers who embark on the path of attempting to create and build culture do so with good intentions, and their hearts are usually in the right place. Even those who don't know where to begin or how to effectively drive culture change want to make a difference and succeed.

Building a great culture takes time and a tremendous amount of energy, which are often far more than you or I can imagine. Not only will it take longer and require far more energy than expected, but the results may not be immediate. I don't mean to sound pessimistic or to instill fear in you about what can happen when leaders and managers become culture fanatics and then dampen your spirits. I only mention this because, while all five of these roadblocks are significant, the third roadblock is what destroys morale and kills momentum gained up to that point.

The reason this temptation is so strong is that I am sure you have read an article or heard something about the importance of culture before you picked up this book. When you start hearing about all the wonderful and great things it can help your organization do, whether it's increasing profit, enhancing performance, or building a top-notch workplace where others want to work, chances are you'll become invigorated. You may be so eager to achieve and accomplish these things that you can't wait to get started. As time passes and the energy you expend outweighs what you receive in return, the adrenaline tends to fade while the comfortable habits of the past begin to take over.

When we have a strong desire for something, our patience is severely tested. Any goal worth achieving, whether it's a personal goal, a professional aspiration, or building a great workplace culture, requires a delicate balance of tenacity and extraordinary patience.

Roadblock #4: Distortion and Distraction

I have witnessed companies that have a committed leadership team as they convert their values and ideas into actionable daily behaviors across the organization. I have watched them create a long-term plan for continuous culture building efforts through speed and impact—and yet, they still fall short of generating the momentum they were hoping for.

Why did this happen?

It seems that once you decide, as a business leader, that you are going to heavily invest in building a better culture, a million ideas and initiatives download into your brain. And it doesn't stop there. Leaders and managers of all levels will put together aggressive action plans so they can present it to the rest of the organization. Once the plan is finished, not only do the leaders start to second-guess themselves and doubt their ability to successfully execute everything on the list, but the second it is presented to the rest of the organization, anxiety takes over. The warning bells start ringing!

Panic attacks.

Heart palpitations.

What were we thinking?

You begin to disconnect. You distract yourself. Remember that shiny object we talked about earlier? You might run right into that. Or everything becomes so overwhelming that you procrastinate and put it off. Then the dysfunction creeps in.

Manifesting a great plan with specific business strategies is extremely important when striving to take your culture to the next level, but beware. Overdoing it and trying to act on too many things at once do the exact opposite of what most leaders want to accomplish. You will shut down. You will have panic overload. Your team will procrastinate. You will lose focus and you will distract yourself by moving to another project without finishing what you started. This becomes a major roadblock when pursuing *Cultural Excellence*.

Take this roadblock seriously. You must use caution when rushing to adopt and implement an idea that you read about, thinking that it will have the exact same effect on your organization. There is a never-ending stream of great ideas and advice in books and articles everywhere you turn. The problem with this is that each organization is unique and has their own set of challenges. Thinking that you can achieve similar results by adopting a best practice another company had great success with is a very dangerous game to play.

There may be an opportunity to integrate parts of different best practices you and your leadership team have collected, but at the end of the day, what worked for someone else won't necessarily work for you or have the same impact that another company might have experienced.

I was in San Francisco a few weeks ago working with the leaders and managers of Hart's Real Estate Firm. I was scheduled to be there for the whole week. I arrived on Sunday afternoon and was going to have dinner with the executive leadership team that evening before the start of a busy week of meetings.

The first hour of our dinner, the fifteen leaders took turns around the table dissecting their biggest troubles with the performance of the company. Fidgeting in their seats, they talked over one another and segued into a monologue about all the details regarding their challenges when it came to creating and building a great culture.

The complaints went on and on.

Dan, the COO of the company, shared with me, "We have tried many different approaches to enhance our business culture;

some things have worked better than others, and some have not. We still haven't experienced the results everyone at this table had hoped for."

"What do you think the problem is?" I asked.

"That's the thing, Matt. We just don't know," said Dan. "We even have a Chief Culture Officer; her name is Jessica, and she's been trying to help us. She's smart and good at what she does. She attends conferences nearly every quarter and visits with other companies to gather best practices. As soon as she comes back and shares some of the ideas with us, we don't waste any time and put it to practice right away. But as time continues, it's clear that we must be doing something wrong because we aren't getting the same results as the company Jessica got the idea from."

Dan, Jessica, and the rest of the leaders at this real estate firm had great intentions of going to conferences and even seeking out best practices that worked well for other companies. But the issue didn't have anything to do with their efforts or desires to build a better culture. The issue was that they didn't take the time to do the discovery work to determine where the major weak points were within their own organization. This is necessary for any company that wants to formulate a prioritized action plan to address the major concerns.

Just throwing ideas around and seeing what sticks and what doesn't isn't going to get you any closer to a solution, and it could actually do more harm than good.

What's the worst thing that could happen, right?

Striving to build and improve your culture to create excellence and the thought that doing something is better than doing nothing, right? Not necessarily. While it is commendable to act, devoting time and energy in the wrong places can be detrimental. The moment more meetings start appearing on calendars and additional activities are added to the daily workload, if the impact isn't connected to driving tangible change, all positive enthusiasm and progress could be lost.

After working with Dan, the COO of Hart's Real Estate, and Jessica, their Chief Culture Officer, I assisted them in developing a plan that was specific to their company's needs and development areas, but it all began with a strong emphasis on where they currently were as an organization rather than throwing around idea after idea.

Dan told me that after a few months, they were seeing improvements not only in employee commitment, but also in the energy that was fostered by having a clear and concise game plan that was tailored to what they needed most.

As a people manager and leader, I encourage you to seek out best practices and read every great book and article that piques your interest. But don't let that distract you from your main goal. Don't let all the reading and task lists prevent you and your team members from devoting the necessary time to identifying the most promising opportunities that will have the greatest impact on where your organization is right now.

Roadblock #5: Lack of Cascading Change

A lack of cascading change throughout the organization is the fifth and final common roadblock to achieving cultural excellence.

And what does cascading change mean in business? The dictionary definition of *cascade* is "a process whereby something, typically information or knowledge, is successively passed on."

Depending on the size of the organization, the difficulty of cascading change will vary. But there is no doubt about it. Building a great culture and changing old organizational habits that no longer serve a company's best interests are extremely difficult work on their own. It is a monumental task to then cascade that change across an entire organization, hoping that men and women of all backgrounds, ages, and personality types will not only buy into the change, but also be a voice of reason.

There needs to be an equal emphasis on strategy and practicality, combined with intuition and a sense of urgency. One of the reasons why cascading cultural change or even taking your current culture to the next level is such a difficult task is because of the existing cultural norms and dynamics that exist within each division and department. Within every organization, there are numerous teams in various divisions and departments. Even if the overall goal for the organization is clear, each team or each department has its own set of beliefs and ways of working. Some of these environments will be overwhelmingly positive, while others will be distressingly negative.

The real challenge in achieving cultural excellence and bringing an entire organization together to move in the same direction is undoing previously learned behaviors and ways of being. Not only that, but then developing and relentlessly implementing a strategic game plan for how communication will be shared, who will say what and when, and presenting a concise breakdown of how the culture will be integrated at scale.

I've seen many leaders and managers do an outstanding job of creating a great culture within their organization, and they prioritize it just like any other critical aspect of the business. However, as time goes on and the journey takes many twists and turns on top of the day-to-day demands of the business, most people are surprised at how difficult it can be to execute large-scale culture change and implementation.

There may be pockets of cultural excellence within the organization, but true cultural excellence requires more than one or three departments living and breathing your culture. Every department, every team member, and every employee understands what the culture is, what it stands for, and how they contribute to bringing the culture to life every day.

It is critical to understand the following in order to achieve this level of execution and understanding throughout the entire organization:

1. Being interested is not the same as action taken. Being interested in creating a great culture is exactly that. Interest. It will never progress unless consistent action is taken.
2. Excellence is an ongoing process with no end goal or finish line. Building a world-class culture that not only allows you to deliver exceptional business results but also provides an environment in which every team member can thrive is a never-ending job.

The organizations and leaders who thrive and succeed in creating this type of culture understand that there is not a typical start or end date like other initiatives or projects. There is only one date when an organization fully commits and then begins to act, and every day after that is a constant pursuit of cultural excellence.

Actions to Mitigate and Overcome the Roadblocks

Let's look at some practical ways to overcome the five common roadblocks to achieving cultural excellence now that we've addressed what the five common roadblocks are. Many of these roadblocks, as well as strategies for mitigating their negative impact, will be discussed in detail in the following chapters.

1. **Overcoming lukewarm leadership buy-in.** You will never have one hundred percent buy-in from all employees, but you can't leave anything to chance with the leadership team. There needs to be a relentless focus—indeed, a *red-hot focus*—on building, growing, and driving a deeper connection among the leadership team from the very beginning. Preferably months before you begin your culture journey, set up frequent and consistent leadership meetings. The objective is to not only create clarity on what the objectives are for the journey ahead but explain why it's important and the pivotal role everyone must play in it. On top of that, it's always a good idea to perform a series of different team building activities. The more you can strengthen trust, be vulnerable with one another, and connect on a personal level, the more it will pay off when it comes to executing and embedding your culture throughout the organization.

2. **Overcoming all slogans and no action:** Focus on turning values into repeatable daily behaviors and integrating your culture into everything you do. Hiring processes, onboarding

programs, leadership development programs, and all company-wide messaging. Being obsessive and attacking your cultural values by being mindful of who is hired, who is let go, and who is eventually promoted sends a strong message of driving expectations moving forward. When your culture becomes a part of you and everything your organization does, you start to remove the "all slogans" and "no action" perception, and it becomes ingrained into your DNA.

3. **Overcoming the temptation of instant gratification:** Over-communicate from the moment you begin building your company's culture and throughout the duration of the process that nothing great is ever created overnight. Establish the standard from the outset. Use anecdotes, illustrations, and analogies to illustrate the consistency and amount of patience required.

4. **Overcoming distortion and distraction:** Organize a 12-month strategy roadmap for how your leadership team will take control of and drive culture. Assemble a committee of highly influential managers and front-line employees to work with the senior leadership team. Decide where you can have the most impact and which cultural actions to focus on first.

5. **Overcoming a lack of cascading change:** In order to keep everyone informed, create a visual communication calendar that lays out what will be communicated to, and cascaded throughout the rest of the organization, and when. Start organizing regular leadership meetings to discuss what is working, what needs to be improved, and which areas of the organization should be given higher priority than others. Never just tell people what your goals or expectations are; be proactive by sending reminders and creating training programs that are tied to specific changes in behavior.

CHAPTER 5

Five Steps to Building a World-Class Culture

Culture guides discretionary behavior and it picks up where the employee handbook leaves off. Culture tells us how to respond to an unprecedented service request. It tells us whether to risk telling our bosses about our new ideas, and whether to surface or hide problems. Employees make hundreds of decisions on their own every day, and culture is our guide. Culture tells us what to do when the CEO isn't in the room, which is of course most of the time.

—Frances Frei and Anne Morriss, co-authors of *Uncommon Service*

You should never apologize for being obsessed with excellence and expecting the best from yourself and those you lead.

"Unfortunately," I said over dinner one night to my friend, Brian, "many of today's business leaders simply miss the mark when it comes to driving culture, and if I were them, I would be obsessed with it."

"What do you mean, Matt?" Brian, a rising manager at a technology consulting firm, took a sip of his beer, then folded his hands on the table and leaned back in his chair. He had just received a promotion and we were celebrating.

"I'm not making a reference to you, Brian. You're doing very well. Overall, I believe it is time for a seismic shift in what is acted upon, rather than simply saying all the right things. If leaders and managers do not constantly reevaluate how to build culture for current and future work environments, and if leaders do not lead the charge, many companies will cease to exist in their current form."

"So, it's all about culture and leadership?"

"Absolutely. Everything starts there. The issue is that many leaders know what they should be doing or communicating all the right points, but there is little action to follow. Obsessive action is needed. A never-ending, driven quest not only to achieve, but to transform from the inside out."

As we were finishing our dinner, Brian told me that his obsession with culture and leadership was what got him promoted, but it also made him feel like an outcast at times. Brian recognized the power of both because of what he had accomplished in just three years. His coworkers thought he was insane and didn't understand his tenacity.

I told Brian what I tell every leader and aspiring manager. If you want to stand out and win in today's competitive environment, you must obsess over building culture and continually seek ways to improve your leadership performance. Tiptoeing around it will never suffice. I make no apologies for my fixation on this.

The author of the business classic, *In Search of Excellence*, Tom Peters, has recently stated, "The hard skills are the soft skills. The soft skills are the hard skills. The time has come."[1]

I couldn't possibly agree more. The old hard skills are valuable, and every leader or aspiring manager should understand them, but I've seen first-hand how soft skills determine a leader's fate and overall impact.

In the long run, this mentality of more companies and leaders building better workplaces could be critical to our economy, the development of future generations, and even our country's future. Just consider this for a moment. If more companies truly prioritized developing their employees as people first and providing an environment in which they could thrive, the benefits would extend beyond the workplace.

As leaders, one by one, we can all work to create this future. In fact, I am confident not only that is it possible for every organization to have a thriving culture that propels their business to new performance heights, but that it should be every leader's mandate. I have devoted my life to helping organizations develop a culture that not only boosts organizational performance but also empowers team members to be the best versions of themselves.

It's astounding what's possible and what starts to happen when an organization's leaders and managers become culture obsessed.

If you've already addressed the roadblocks I mentioned in Chapter 4, it's time to start working on developing (or rebuilding) your company's culture. Remember, as a leader and manager, you must approach culture-building as you would any other critical aspect of an organization, where previous limitations and barriers must be removed.

I've seen struggling businesses completely transform into world-class organizations. There have been other examples of companies that have been successful for the past decade but have been unable to surpass their current level of success. All of that

changed when leaders focused relentlessly on shepherding behaviors, teamwork, and alignment to build and/or rebuild their
culture, which propelled them to new heights.

There is no one-size-fits-all solution for developing or improving an organization's culture. This is because each organization is unique, with specific needs and areas for development.
A positive and strong culture may already exist in one organization, while another is in desperate need of a complete cultural
transformation. Another organization may have new management with the goal of revamping and setting a new direction for
the company. While some businesses have a strong foundation,
certain aspects of their current culture require more attention
and development than other areas.

I've been involved in hundreds of different instances over
the last decade in which business leaders are desperately seeking the best and most effective way to improve their culture
and individual leadership. I've been incredibly fortunate to
have had a front-row seat to some of the world's most influential corporations. So, after years of experimenting, copious
research, and merging key learnings from my days as an athlete
on the football field, I formulated five steps for building and
sustaining a world-class culture (Figure 5.1). Although several
iterations of this process have been employed, mostly in medium and large-sized corporations, they can be adapted for any
organization, profit or nonprofit.

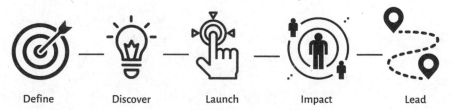

| Define | Discover | Launch | Impact | Lead |

FIGURE 5.1   The Five-Step Culture-Building Process

The Five-Step Process

Step One: Define Your Culture

If you ask a group of people who appear to work for the same company while you're out and about on the street, "What is the culture of your company?," most likely, each respondent will have a different answer. In thriving and world-class enterprises, everyone knows what the culture is, what it stands for, and what's expected of them within that organization. Further on in this book, we will create a cultural purpose statement in this stage of the process, which is an important first step in defining what your culture stands for. This cultural purpose statement will serve as a foundation for everything else and will aid in organizational alignment.

Step Two: Discovery Through Collaboration and Inspiration

The discovery phase focuses on a collaborative and inspirational approach that engages the entire organization in the culture-building process. Senior leaders will collaborate and partner with all people managers in the organization, soliciting specific feedback along the way to encourage and highlight valuable employee input. Collaboration between the senior leadership team and all people managers is extremely powerful in and of itself, but the impact is greatly increased when the process shifts to a bottom-up approach. As important as senior leaders are when it comes to large-scale change in an organization, this collaborative and inspirational approach is far more effective because it inspires managers and other key stakeholders to become more committed. Unless all leaders and front-line managers, as well as employees, have a strong commitment, the results will be minimal.

Step Three: Launch, Cascade, and Embed

It is detrimental to the organization as a whole if the culture does not trickle down from the top and permeate all departments. Many leaders and people managers believe that it is enough if a company has strong core values and defines its culture openly. But it isn't. Leaders must make it a priority to disseminate it across the entire organization. This stage of the process is all about launching and relentlessly implementing it across the rest of the company, as well as embedding it across all functions. In the absence of a strategy for propagating your culture, you run the risk of it remaining isolated and having little impact.

Step Four: Drive Long-Term Impact

It is one thing to create a momentary buzz about your culture, which can have a short-term effect; it is quite another to create a culture that embodies the core DNA of your organization and has a lasting impact. Some businesses may see instant results from a one-time advertising campaign that generates excitement for a short period of time, but the true test is whether those businesses can create a culture of sustainability that produces ongoing innovation and long-term impact. This stage of the process aids in reducing the likelihood that your culture will only have a short-term impact and helps you develop a strategy for creating a sustainable culture that consistently delivers for your organization.

Step Five: Leaders Must Blaze the Trail

This final stage of the process is a deciding factor in whether an organization succeeds or fails in its pursuit of creating a world-class culture. It all comes down to how well an organization's leaders model the way forward, practice what they preach daily, set clear cultural expectations for everyone to abide by, and blaze the trail forward. What leaders do on a regular basis, and how they behave, send a strong message to the organization. Even when leaders believe others in the company are not watching, employees are acutely aware of what is being communicated. They observe how everything is reflected in their leaders' daily actions. Communicating a culture change or your desire to build a better one will always fall by the wayside without a strong leadership team leading the way forward and establishing the tone.

Finally, I will say to all of you, *"Lead! Just lead! You can make the ground beneath your feet rumble with excitement, energy, and ongoing incremental progress by blazing the trail forward."*

CHAPTER 6

Create Your Cultural Purpose Statement

Group culture is one of the most powerful forces on the planet.

—Daniel Coyle, *The Culture Code*

I jolted forward in my seat, anxious to get moving.

As we came to an abrupt stop, the captain said, "Welcome to Chicago, where the sky is overcast and rainy and the temperature is 42 degrees Fahrenheit and 5.5 degrees Celsius. Hope you have a pleasant stay and thank you for flying Delta Airlines!"

Overcast. Rainy. I would have expected nothing less. This was my Chicago, my home, and it rained a lot.

There was a great clatter of luggage being hauled out of overhead bins as the passengers jumped up, preparing to exit the plane. I grabbed my small carryon, ready to step into the aisle and head for the exit door. It felt good to stretch my legs.

When the door opened, and the flight attendant motioned all of us to move forward, I ran out and rushed through O'Hare Airport to make my way to a local hotel in Downtown Chicago, where I was scheduled to give another talk. Time was tight, so I didn't have an opportunity to grab lunch, let alone stop at home to refresh for my next engagement.

It was 2018, and I was three months into my partnership with Southern Glazer's Wine and Spirits of Illinois (SGWS-IL). For the first few months of our partnership, I worked with the senior leadership team, strategizing new processes and programs centered around enhancing the leadership performance of the senior team. To begin our meeting, we engaged in a round of brainstorming and asked each other:

- Where are we as an organization now, and where do we aspire to be in a year or two?
- How can we shift into a higher paradigm for growth, development, market share, and profitability?
- What mindset and behavioral shifts are needed to make this paradigm shift happen?

As we learned in Chapter 4, one of the five common roadblocks to achieving cultural excellence is leadership complacency or "Lukewarm Leadership Buy-In."

Regardless of which organization I'm working with or how positive or negative their current workplace culture is, one of my first priorities is to spend isolated time with the senior leadership team. Along with starting to build a more connected and effective senior leadership team, the focus is on laying the groundwork for how important culture is.

SGWS-IL was a unique case. They had been performing at an extremely high level for quite some time. Their commercial success was inspiring, and it was easy to see why as time passed. For one thing, they were obsessed with commercial execution and always moved at lightning speed. They were determined to not only achieve their goals but also give their customers and suppliers an exceptional experience.

I say it was a unique case because they never had a major performance issue. Sure, there were areas for improvement, but plenty of others would probably consider nothing alarming enough to devote so much time and effort to leadership development and culture.

After a productive discussion about the brainstorming questions that we started the meeting with, I then asked, "What is your culture here at SGWS-IL?"

After a few blank stares, leaders in the room started to shout out different ideas of what they thought the culture was. Some leaders were quick to reference the company's FAMILY Values, while others recited the written corporate mission and vision statements. Other leaders used strong, dominant phrases that they thought perfectly captured the essence of what made the company special. Words like:

Excellence

Commitment

Execution

Good words. But, also, *ho-hum* words that could be found on placards anywhere and everywhere, from airports to gift shops. Words that could make you yawn and your eyes glaze over with boredom.

No one could argue that any of these suggestions were completely wrong, though. As a matter of fact, most of the suggestions shared that afternoon were a part of who the company was and what made them unique.

But what was interesting was that there wasn't a clear definitive response from those twenty leaders that afternoon. Everyone had their own definition of what the culture was.

As the leaders shared their suggestions with me, I took notes and wrote down everything they said. After about ten minutes, I asked, "Do you realize what just happened? Even though all of you shared what you thought made this organization special and the culture here, I have 35 different things written down on this piece of paper."

They all looked at one another with blank expressions on their faces.

I continued, "Great cultures are defined cultures. This means that every leader, manager, and employee can describe the culture and what it stands for, and the descriptions will be very similar to a large extent."

Again, they all looked at one another, some with brows furrowed.

"Think about this for a minute," I said. "Perhaps you've never looked at it this way."

A few people conversed quietly among themselves. After a few minutes, Terry Brick, whom I introduced in Chapter 4, said, "Matt, this makes perfect sense and is exactly what we need. We have a set of values that we call our FAMILY Values, but as we discovered today, everyone interprets our culture differently. We must define it."

This is something I come across often. When asked to define their culture, a leader or a group of employees from various departments will begin by sharing their core values, mission statement, or some inspiring words that they believe best represent their culture.

When that question is asked, it's rare to find a group of team members who react in a consistent manner, reciting the same definition of what their culture is and what it stands for.

Any organization, like SGWS-IL, can achieve success and commercial excellence without a defined culture, but untapped potential may be lying dormant.

Creating clarity and defining your organizational culture form one of the first steps toward achieving cultural excellence that will produce extraordinary results and drive real business impact. Remember that a company's core values, mission and vision statements, and everything else on its website are all aspects of its culture. A minor aspect at that.

This isn't to say that all companies that don't have a defined culture have a *bad* culture. SGWS-IL had a stellar culture, but it was somewhat stagnant and not clearly defined to help the company progress and evolve the way they needed to. During my global travels, I've come across many organizations that have a healthy and high-performing culture, even if it wasn't defined at the time. However, if the goal is to build an organization that continually shatters limitations and achieves excellence, defining your culture is essential.

It is extremely powerful to have a clear, defined, and concise cultural purpose statement that serves as a guiding force for everything you do.

Creating a Cultural Purpose Statement

During that meeting in Chicago in 2018, the SGWS-IL senior leaders and I spent the next three hours strategizing about various ideas for their cultural purpose statement. The group was comfortable opening up and sharing their opinions because we had already been working together for a few months and had established a regular cadence.

Just as we were about to wrap up, Terry Brick shared with the team, "Matt introduced the motto, 'Get Better Today,' during our last meeting and how important it is to incorporate that mindset as leaders. That motto has resonated with us ever since then, so what if we add the word *together* at the end and adopt that as our *cultural purpose statement*?"

A chorus of shouts rang out through the room:

"I love it!"

"Hey, I'm good with that!"

"Nothing can stop us if we truly live and abide by this. I'm on board!"

"I just think it describes us perfectly," Terry concluded the meeting after other leaders at the meeting agreed with his suggestion. "It explains who we are, where we want to go, and what we need to do as leaders and as a team to achieve our SGWS FAMILY's mission. It also paves the way for producing outstanding results for our suppliers and customers. I am confident that if we 'Get Better Today. . .Together,' we will achieve and accomplish everything we set out to do."

To my surprise, we left that meeting not only with that cultural purpose statement selected, but also with renewed enthusiasm. The senior executives were on fire! The excitement and energy were palpable. All because of four simple words: *Get Better Today. . .Together*!

Fast forward to March 2020, when the global pandemic hit. Those four words were a powerful catalyst, allowing SGWS-IL not only to survive the pandemic, but also to thrive and have one of their best years ever.

Did this cultural purpose statement of "Get Better Today. . . Together" change everything in an instant? Was it solely responsible for them navigating the complexity of the pandemic and thriving? Of course not. But what it did was provide clarity for defining their culture and offer them a new paradigm to attack each day with excitement and passion. *When they were tested by the crisis, it sparked hope and connected them deeper to their mission, all while focusing on the process of daily improvement.*

And in time, "Get Better Today. . .Together," became embedded into the hearts and minds of employees at scale. It became their cultural North Star. That's the power of a cultural purpose statement and what it can do. A statement, motto, theme, whatever you wish to call it. However, this statement has the potential to instill tremendous energy and alignment around what an organization does, how well it does it, and, most importantly, how it responds in every situation.

When asked about the culture of their workplace, a team member will be able to respond without missing a beat. The cultural purpose statement not only helps define and drive clarity around your culture, but it also has the potential to make a profound difference in the personal lives of every team member.

Selecting a word, slogan, or mantra and simply using it as lip service because it sounds good will not do much or benefit anyone. Using SGWS-IL as an example, and their cultural purpose statement of "Get Better Today. . .Together," part of the reason it had such an impact was that it wasn't just applied to their business or the professional lives of their employees. If you're a father, you can take advantage of the practicality of that statement by actively looking for ways to improve for that day with your children. If a team member is passionate about community service and making a difference, they can adopt the statement by inviting others to join them in improving the lives of others and their local communities.

I recently had two very inspiring conversations with managers at SGWS-IL on the impact that "Get Better Today. . .Together" had on their personal lives.

Joshua

The first example was Joshua, a team member who had been with the company for over twenty years. At the time, Joshua was going through a very difficult phase of his life. He was the primary caregiver for a parent who had recently passed away.

At the same time, the pandemic was starting to take an emotional toll on him and all his family. "I have to be honest with you, Matt," said Joshua one day when we were talking on the phone, "when the leadership team started talking about 'Get Better Today. . .Together,' I thought it was going to just be another tag line, another slogan, that would be bandied about for a couple of months and then we'd move on to another phrase like we had always done."

The emotion in his voice was palpable and he paused, stifling tears. I understood what he was feeling and gave him space to get his thoughts together.

Finally, Joshua continued, "As time went on and I saw that this time, the slogan wasn't a temporary thing, it really pulled me out of the gutter. 'Get Better Today. . .Together' became such an uplifting, inspiring way of life as time went on. We were one team. We were in this together! Suddenly, I didn't feel so alone in my life. Know what I mean, Matt?"

"Yeah, I do." Briefly, my emotions began to take over as I recalled my time in football with Coach Hep, who first coined the term, "Get Better Today," and I remembered how lonely I felt when he passed away.

"Matt, this is not some small thing. I am not sure I would have been able to get over the loss of someone very close to me and keep pressing forward without practicing it daily, along with people I worked with."

Edward

It was a pale, gray day in downtown Chicago when I joined Edward, from SGWS-IL, in a Parisian-style café. He was already there, quietly sipping an espresso and enjoying the "little taste" of Europe, which the café was known for. The aromas of piping-hot roasted coffee and fresh-baked local pastries wafted pleasantly through the café.

When I entered the door, I waved at him, then grabbed a coffee from the counter and joined him at his table. Edward, who was retiring soon, had called earlier, and asked if we could talk over coffee for a few minutes. He said he had an interesting story to tell me. "Of course," I told him.

At this time of day, we mostly had the café to ourselves.

"How you doin' today?" I asked Edward when I joined him at his table.

"Good. Good. Thanks for coming out to meet me," he said.

"Sure." I scooted my chair closer to the table and took a sip of the coffee.

"Matt, you wanna know something? I've always been terrified of retiring because I love the company I work for. My wife died a couple of years ago, and my two children live in California, so it's mostly just me and my dog, Scottie. I have always believed I would be lost without my job. But because of you and our leadership team, I have been applying our cultural purpose statement, 'Get Better Today. . .Together,' to my personal life."

"Personally?" I asked.

"Uh-huh. It's helped me to find ways to expand my life and pursue hobbies that I had never considered before."

"So glad to hear that, Ed," I said. "Can you be more specific?"

"This statement reminded me that I am not alone. That there are others in this world who will share my ideas and passions, and whom I can build a new community with, even after retiring."

I smiled. "You are absolutely correct."

"I've been looking for hobbies and things to do when the time comes for me to retire. The cultural purpose statement has helped me get out of my comfort zone and try new things every day after work and on weekends. After a year, I know exactly what I want to do and with whom I want to do it."

Ed pulled out a binder and showed me two pages that detailed his post-retirement plan.

Ed's eyes were welling up with tears. "All I've ever known is work. Working for Southern. I enjoy the fast-paced environment. I never imagined I'd find something to fill that void in my life when it came time for me to leave."

These are just two examples, but there are countless others of how this cultural purpose statement impacted not only employees' professional lives, but also their personal lives.

Lessons from College Football Coaches

There are some excellent examples from college football when discussing the significance of identifying and creating a cultural purpose statement and using that as the North Star for your culture.

In Chapter 1, I mentioned that some of the best culture-builders are coaches in the sports world. I believe there are a few reasons for this. An elite college football coach faces a different opponent each week who is determined to dominate their team. The opponent spends the entire week leading up to the game that week dissecting your every weakness.

One week you are on top of the world and a star, and the next week you are enemy number one, even in your own home state. The local media scrutinizes your every move and criticizes *everything* that you say or do when you are not winning games. There is no such thing as even remotely close to having job security, and sometimes the public may find out you're fired even before you do.

Not to mention, every week there is a scorecard on your performance for the public to see. A winner and loser are decided on the spot each Saturday, and then there is a video of your performance for everyone to view. It can be demeaning and humiliating. Embarrassing. Or it can be wonderful and exhilarating if you're one of the winning star coaches that week.

There are similarities in the business world as a leader and manager. It is extremely demanding, difficult, and can be brutal and cutthroat. There are shareholders and board members whom leaders must report to. Customers can be just as relentless. The demands from them are constantly evolving and changing, while the changes occurring inside and outside of the organization can be overwhelming at the same time.

As a leader and people manager in the business world, your minute-by-minute performance every day is not necessarily being recorded and played on the news every night. At least not in an obvious way. When a mistake or costly decision is made in business, it could take months or even years for the public to hear about it.

Even though key stakeholders and leaders in business want to win *now* and often place great urgency behind their ambitions, the demand to win *immediately* is not the same as what's required of elite college football coaches.

I'm not comparing the importance or even the difficulty of elite college football coaches and business leaders. Both jobs are extremely difficult and demanding, but the dynamics and expectations are very different.

That is why I believe football coaches are excellent examples of the intensity, commitment, and consistency needed to create a winning and thriving culture. They must win now, and there is little time to waste. The only way to unite 100 young men from diverse backgrounds, experiences, intellect levels, and personalities is to clearly define the football program's culture, which serves as its foundation. Not to mention that almost all these athletes have an ego, or they would not have made it to an elite college football program in the first place.

It is the goal of every major college football program to win their conference championship. Setting goals and envisioning where you want to go are important, but every other team is doing the same.

Culture is the primary differentiator. Coaches must win right away, and the best understand that the results and daily behaviors they desire from their players begin with the environment and culture they create and demand daily. Let's look at some specific examples of college football coaches who have used the power of creating a cultural purpose statement, anchor statement, or mantra not only to build a great culture but also to produce exceptional results on the field.

Mel Tucker, "Relentless," Michigan State Spartans Head Coach

It doesn't matter if it's business or sports, great leaders are relentless in their pursuits. Take Mel Tucker, for example. Mel Tucker was hired in February 2020 as the head football coach for the Michigan State Spartans. At the time, most college football projections had the Spartans finishing at the bottom of the Big Ten conference. While 2020 was a difficult year for them, one year later the Spartans became a legitimate contender for a birth into the College Football Playoff and they finished the 2021 season with an 11-2 overall record.

What was the deciding factor in this extraordinary turnaround? They were relentless! This was the culture that Coach

Tucker instilled in his team. An attitude of "never give up." A daily practice consisting of drills that constantly emphasized improvement, whether in the huddle or while pursuing the football. And attention to detail. Chin straps were buckled, shoes were tied, and shirts were tucked in.[1]

"Culture is everything," Coach Tucker has said in many press conferences. He promised the fan base on the first day he took over as head coach that they could expect an improved and winning culture. The word "relentless" became the foundation of everything the Spartans did, resulting in an improved and winning culture. Coach Tucker's use of the word "relentless" may appear to be a catchphrase or buzzword, but it serves a much larger purpose, as shown by their performance thus far.

Tom Allen, L.E.O. "Love Each Other," Indiana Hoosiers Head Coach

Tom Allen isn't worried about anyone thinking that L.E.O. is corny. It's his motto, his anchor statement. Wherever Tom Allen goes, one can hear him shout the initials L.E.O. at any given time. This acronym stands for "Love Each Other" and is the backbone of the Indiana culture that Tom Allen has built. You might ask, "How in the world does loving one another help a football team win, especially in a violent sport such as football?"

Coach Allen has an answer. While speaking at an event for the Illinois High School Football Coaches Association Coach Allen said, "What does love have to do with football? Everything. I will love you so much that I won't allow mediocrity from you."[2]

Many players admitted that, at first, they didn't know what to make of all the L.E.O. talk, with some mistaking it for a new teammate or astrological sign. They were amused to learn that it was an acronym for "love each other," but they trusted Coach Allen, who told them that one must have the proper mindset before reality can take hold. That meant that before the team could begin to improve and win on the field, the players needed to build mutual trust, respect, and even affection for one another.[3]

As time went on and Coach Allen continued to passionately instill L.E.O in every facet of the program, the players not only started to understand its importance, but results on the field followed. For the first time since 1969, the Hoosiers were ranked top 10 in the AP poll during the 2020 season, recording wins over Michigan, Penn State, and Wisconsin.

Nick Saban, "The Process," Alabama Crimson Tide

Nick Saban is one of the greatest college football coaches of all time, and some may argue that he is one of the greatest coaches of all time in any sport. He holds the most coaching titles in college football history, and his team's consistency year after year is nothing short of remarkable. Is this because Nick Saban can recruit and bring in some of the best high school football players in the country? Definitely. However, talent will only get you so far. His attention to detail and unwavering preparation are unrivaled.

His program is built on what he refers to as "The Process." It has been well documented that if you walk the halls of the Alabama facility, you will rarely see goals of winning a national championship.

Coach Saban has often said that if one focuses solely on the end result and does not put in the necessary preparation, they will lose. Focusing on what needs to be done each day to achieve success is at the heart of Saban's process mentality, rather than a specific goal. One must decide on the standard they want to strive for, follow that standard, and then put that standard into practice every day.[4]

For Coach Saban, "The Process" isn't just a saying that he repeats over and over in interviews with the media or preaches to his team. It's something that he not only lives every day of his life but also demands of his players and staff. The difference between winning and losing is in the details. Focusing on "The Process" serves as a constant reminder for Coach Nick Saban and his Alabama Crimson Tide. "Becoming a champion is not an easy process. It is done by focusing on what it takes to get there and not on getting there."

P.J. Fleck, "Row the Boat," Minnesota Golden Gophers

Much has been written about Coach P.J. Fleck, the current head football coach of the Minnesota Golden Gophers. Coach Fleck is known for his fiery, passionate coaching style. On any given Saturday, you'll see Coach Fleck running up and down the sidelines faster than most of his players, yelling and pleading with them to go, go, go! After that, you'll see him sprinting over to congratulate his players when they make a big play.

Coach Fleck coined his mantra, "Row the Boat," after a personal tragedy. He lost his newborn son due to a heart condition, and as devastating as that loss was, Coach Fleck sought to understand the deeper meaning of it all. He began to reflect on how most people stop rowing when adversity strikes and compared one's ability to move forward depending on whether the oars are left in the water or brought back into the boat.

When Coach Fleck first introduced his "Row the Boat" mantra and, with it, built a strong football culture, the media and the general public began to wonder if he was more of a motivational speaker than a football coach. He wrote about his theme, his coaching mantra, in *Row the Boat*, a book he coauthored with bestselling author Jon Gordon. And Coach Fleck has his own video coaching series. His mantra is described in both the book and the video series as follows:

- *The Oar: The energy*. Only you can dictate whether your oar is in the water or whether you take it out and decide not to use it.
- *The Boat: The sacrifice*. The more you give, serve, and make your life about helping others, the better and more fulfilled your life will be, and the bigger your boat gets.
- *The Compass: The direction*. The vision you have for your life and the people you surround yourself with help create the dream of where you want to go.

Coach Fleck has said that the "Row the Boat" process describes how his entire football program works. This is a motivating message about what you can do when you approach life with a "Row the Boat" mentality. Business leaders in any organization or company can use this same type of thinking to achieve success.[5]

Much More Than a Clever Mantra

Even though the college football coaches I've mentioned may not refer to these descriptions as their cultural purpose statement, they all achieve the same thing. Every one of these teams has a defining word, statement, or mantra that is woven into every aspect of their football program. If you were to dig a little deeper into their stories, you will quickly realize that this is not just a clever mantra for them. It is absolutely everything to them. Like Coach Fleck, who created his "Row the Boat" theme after losing a newborn son. All of these head coaches look to their North Star for guidance on how to manage their football program. They instruct their teams on what is expected of everyone in the program, and their mantra serves as a compass for each player, both on and off the field.

You can do the same thing within your company.

There are a few misconceptions that I hear from business leaders when I introduce the idea of creating a cultural purpose statement that will help define your culture.

A few things to keep in mind:

1. **Don't be confused:** The cultural purpose statement should not be confused with a mission or vision statement. Even though some companies have replaced their current mission or vision statement with their cultural purpose statement over time, this is not the point. Instead, it's designed to help your organization's culture be defined and its fundamental foundation be made crystal clear. I was helping an organization in the financial services industry execute a major cultural change. During one of our leadership meetings, one of

their executives said, "Is that the best use of our time? We already have a mission statement. Here, look on the back of this brochure." He pushed it in front of me and I looked at it, then asked the rest of the 60 leaders in the room, "How many of you would recite this mission statement off the top of your head if someone asked what the culture is here?" The executive who originally asked me if this was the proper use of their time looked around the room, waiting for hands to go up. Not one hand went up out of the 60 senior leaders in one room. "And that is why we need to create a cultural purpose statement," I said.

2. **One step in the journey:** Choosing a cultural purpose statement is just one step in the journey of creating a better culture and work environment. Unfortunately, I've watched leaders and management teams who, upon selecting a cultural purpose statement, became elated, believing that the hard work had been completed. Uh, no. As you read in earlier chapters and will continue to read throughout the rest of this book, one step or one aspect of the process will never build or change a culture on its own. As important as it is to define your culture and choose a word or mantra that will serve as the foundation for your culture, you must also understand and constantly remind team members that it is only one step in the right direction. When we act on something as important as cultural change, it's easy to confuse progress with the "we're done" attitude and then move on to the next thing. Declaring victory too soon not only creates extra problems, but it can also destroy all earlier progress to change culture.

3. **No agreement needed:** You don't need unanimous agreement when deciding on your cultural purpose statement. In the early stages of any change initiative, complete agreement is unlikely, and focusing on the belief that it is needed often causes indecision and slows down many leadership teams. Driving collaboration and engaging the rest of the organization throughout the culture-building process is important and will be covered in detail in forthcoming chapters. Right

now, the most important thing is to make sure that the leadership team is aligned. Depending on the size of an organization, it may make sense to include other departments, but the wider and larger that sphere becomes, indecision becomes more prevalent. Over the years, I have found that the more people who are included in creating a cultural purpose statement, the slower the decision-making process. Leaders lead. And for that reason, you, as the leader, should define the company's cultural purpose statement. Things begin to fall into place when leaders are committed to the cause and are able to explain how it all fits into the bigger picture.

Create Your Own Cultural Purpose Statement

There are lessons to be learned from others and examples to be inspired by, but it's important to remember that your cultural purpose statement should be unique to your organization. Before you begin the process of defining your culture, there are many factors to consider and examine. Even though your cultural purpose statement should be something that the leadership team is passionate about and fully supports, there are a variety of conditions that should help you along the way.

For example, if an organization recently went through a merger and employee morale is low and negative, this should be considered during the examination phase. If an organization is experiencing tremendous growth but still has lofty and ambitious growth plans for the coming year, a different level of analysis is needed.

When Michael Thompson was the head of operations at SGWS-IL, he was one of the leaders I worked closely with. I mentioned earlier that he was one of the brightest leaders I had ever met, and his intelligence and strong leadership abilities paid off when he was tasked with taking over the state of Indiana as

General Manager. SGWS-IN was in a completely different situation than Illinois. It was a high-performing organization, but there were many disparate dynamics and challenges to consider. To give some context, they had gone through a merger five years prior, and there had been turnover in key leadership positions over the years. Because of these events, morale and excitement for the organization's future were not where they needed to be.

When I first started working with Mike and the SGWS-IN team, we focused on defining the culture with a cultural purpose statement. Thompson and the SGWS-IN team ultimately chose "Inspiring the Future Together" as their cultural purpose statement.

They chose this not only because of where the organization was and how everyone felt at the time, but also because of where they wanted to take the organization in the future. They had to create excitement and inspire every employee with the idea that the future of SGWS-IN would be bigger and better than it had been in the past. They also shared that, as a group, they needed to inspire customers and suppliers by delivering exceptional experiences and results. Based on their demonstrated abilities—where they were and where they wanted to take the company—this cultural purpose statement was in alignment with both their short-term and long-term goals.

There was extensive thought and energy put into where they were as an organization.

Consider the following questions when guiding your organization's leadership team in discovering its own cultural purpose statement:

1. What do we deeply care about as an organization, both internally and externally?
2. Where are we now and where do we want to be?
3. What must happen to bridge the gap between where we are and where we want to be?
4. What do we want our culture to stand for?
5. What is our culture's most significant impact area?

FIGURE 6.1 What Great Cultural Purpose Statements Provide

6. How would we like our culture to be perceived?

7. What experience do we hope our culture will provide?

8. What mantras or statements best summarize our call to action?

9. Can we, as leaders, live up to this mantra or statement daily?

10. Can this mantra or statement benefit not only our business but also our personal lives?

Figure 6.1 shows what a great cultural purpose statement should do for you and your organization.

Action Steps for Leaders

The steps that follow will help you define your organization's culture and create your own cultural purpose statement. These steps can serve as a roadmap for your future journey, whether you want to completely change your culture or take your current culture to the next level.

1. Schedule not one, but two or three meetings with the senior leadership team in case you require more time. Don't make the mistake of thinking you can fit this part into an already mandated meeting. Each of these meetings should have their

own theme and agenda. When it is tacked onto other meetings, there is almost never enough time, and the process is rushed.

2. Develop a pre-read to send out via email to all the leaders who are attending a week before the scheduled meetings. In the pre-read email, clearly state the meeting's objective, why the meeting is being held, and clarify the tone for the dynamics of the meeting.

3. Encourage group participation and an open discussion meeting format. The leader should address the team at the start to lay the groundwork for the importance of defining the culture and collaborating on a cultural purpose statement. Then return the focus back to the group and open it up for discussion.

4. Ensure that everyone stays on track and focused on the task at hand. It's very possible, and not uncommon, for the conversation to veer off topic or for someone to go on a rant about a specific issue.

5. Once the group has chosen a cultural purpose statement, relentlessly begin sharing it and explaining its significance at every opportunity. There will be a more formal roll-out of this in the following chapters, but you can begin communicating it now.

CHAPTER 7

Winning Hearts and Minds for Impactful Culture-Building

No matter how brilliant your mind or strategy, if you're playing a solo game, you'll always lose out to a team.

—Reid Hoffman

In 2012, Google was pursuing a determined path to study and analyze the hundreds of different teams within the organization and get to the bottom of why some teams succeeded and why others fell short. The company-wide initiative was dubbed *Project Aristotle* in honor of Aristotle's quote, "The whole is greater than the sum of its parts."[1]

Researchers at Google figured that employees would be more productive if they collaborated rather than worked alone. "What makes a team effective at Google?" was the ultimate question they wanted to answer. They decided to assess the performance of their most successful teams and replicate their success by forming similar teams throughout the organization. After years of extensive research and analyzing the data gathered from nearly 200 interviews with different teams at Google, they discovered multiple key characteristics that make a great team, but psychological safety was the most important.[2]

Psychological safety can mean different things to different people. Amy Edmonson, the author of *The Fearless Organization* and Novartis Professor of Leadership and Management at Harvard Business School, says: "Psychological safety isn't about being nice. It's about giving candid feedback, openly admitting mistakes, and learning from each other."[3]

There has been a lot of discussion about psychological safety over the years but based on my experience working with organizations and leadership teams in a variety of industries, I believe there is still a gap. The disconnect between leaders occurs when they recognize the significance of psychological safety but do not put in the effort required to cultivate it within their organizations and teams. *What good is it to know something valuable if you don't take steps to implement it?*

Those in leadership positions are not always to blame. For many leaders, especially those with decades of experience and those who are accustomed to leading and managing in a certain manner, behaviors of the past become more ingrained with time. In addition, it is more complicated for larger organizations to effectively enhance employee engagement and create a sense of psychological safety.

What does this have to do with culture? It's simple. To effectively build, rebuild, or change culture, there must be a deliberate focus on engaging the organization in completely new, innovative ways. That is another area where psychological safety comes into the picture and what Google discovered when they began to identify the core characteristics of their best teams.

Regardless of what the end goal is, improving or successfully changing culture is predicated on the level of commitment from leaders to engage the hearts and minds of all employees. An organization's culture won't drastically change or improve if the voice of the individual employee is not highlighted. Significant and lasting change can only materialize when employees feel comfortable enough to speak up while being encouraged that their opinion matters. When knowing that leaders *listen* in the hopes of truly making things better, the employees will become more communicative and open about sharing their hearts and minds regarding work. This is psychological safety.

In toxic cultures where psychological safety is not present, employees are not only less likely to speak up, but when they do, they will be more inclined to say what they *think* leaders want to hear. Maybe they only mimic what they think the leaders want to hear out of a fear of being punished, fired, or shunned. This only obfuscates the whole purpose of understanding what's needed because if employees lie, leaders will never know the real truth. As a result, they will never be able to create and manifest real change and impact.

I recently advised the senior leadership team of a large insurance company in the early stages of their culture change process. For about four months, we had been holding regular leadership meetings to lay the groundwork for their culture change journey.

Every senior leader in the organization agreed that a change was necessary because employees were not fully engaged in giving feedback. For example, the company scored below average in annual employee engagement surveys for three years in a row, with one of the lowest scores centered on fear. Employees were too afraid to speak up.

When we strategized about implementing key action steps, one of the primary focus areas was to engage employees and seek feedback in a way they had never done before. Instead of waiting for the standard annual employee engagement survey to be completed, we decided that leaders should make an intentional effort to engage, communicate, and listen to employees every step of the way.

The journey to culture change is seldom easy.

When Ron, a senior leader who has been instrumental in the company's success over the last seven years, first heard about the idea, he was hesitant. "One of the reasons we have been successful and do great work for our clients is because of the speed with which we move and operate. Listening to people simply complain about what they don't like will cause us to slow down."

I listened to some of Ron's colleagues chime in. Some agreed, some disagreed.

Finally, I responded to his remarks, "Ron, you are correct. You've always been known for your speed and urgency, but not only are you losing key people because of the troubled areas we discussed this morning, but these issues will only worsen from here. Doing things differently and engaging the organization in a deeper and more profound way will benefit operations and allow you to move even faster."

Ron wasn't completely sold after that meeting, or even a few months afterwards for that matter. Eventually, he came around, though, and I'm proud to say that nowadays we joke about his reluctance to change.

I'm sharing this example with you because the mindset and perspective that Ron fostered toward engaging and listening to employees are very common, and they become a very troubling obstacle for companies on their culture change journey.

I have heard it all. Leaders believe it is not only a waste of time, but also that they already know what employees will complain about, so why bother asking them? Other leaders believe that culture change, or any organizational change initiative, should not be open to input and suggestions from anyone other than senior leaders. Some leaders have even expressed concern that it may send the wrong message to employees, making the leaders appear weak.

Organizations and companies do not change by themselves or because their leaders express a desire to do so. Organizations and companies do not change. Those who change are the people who work in those organizations: the employees. Mindsets and behaviors must be changed before the culture can be changed. Changing culture begins with changing one person's mindset and behavior at a time. And changing mindsets and behaviors, especially at scale, necessitates making people feel like they are a vital part of the process rather than relying on old engagement methods.

In Chapter 6, when I talked about how important it is to create a cultural purpose statement, I noted that the leaders of an organization should define their culture and show the way forward. Once the culture is defined, it's important to shift gears and change the mindsets and behaviors of employees by placing a strong emphasis on intentionally engaging the rest of the organization.

Leaders and managers at all levels play an integral role in driving employee engagement. According to research, leaders and all people managers account for at least 70% of engagement levels.[4] Continuous conversations between leaders and employees are essential for keeping them on track and feeling supported. How can a leader influence and change mindsets if they don't know what their employees are thinking? Management must constantly communicate priorities, highlight important goals, solicit feedback, and remove roadblocks as they arise.

Top-Down Directed, but Bottom-Up Created

Many culture change initiatives fall flat because only a small number of leaders are responsible for the majority of the journey's direction and execution. If others are included in the process, it is because it has been delegated to a committee or Human

Resources. Most of the time, it is not a collaborative journey in which all voices are heard, all opinions are shared, and all input is encouraged. However, it should be. That is where the process of true transformation and change begins.

At the end of 2021, I gave a 60-minute speech to Direct Federal Credit Union which was focused on leadership and culture. At the end, we opened it up for fifteen minutes of Q&A.

Joe Walsh is the CEO of Direct Federal. Before employees began asking questions, Joe shared a few changes he made in real time during my presentation on one of the company's core values and a few tweaks to the upcoming culture plan. I'm not telling you this to brag about how good my speech was that day, but to emphasize how important culture was to Joe and how he was always looking for ways to improve it. I was so impressed with Joe's leadership and commitment to building culture after that event. I recently had a great conversation with him about the balancing act of leaders driving culture while also involving employees in the process.

"What was the one decision you made since you took over in 2014 as CEO that has positively shaped your culture?" I asked him.

"Something that's hard to do for most leaders when it comes to culture is giving up what feels like control. But something that I have learned over my career is that culture needs to be top-down *directed* but then bottom-up *created*."

"Interesting. I like that concept."

"My job as CEO," Joe continued, "and something I tell all our senior leaders is that our main job is to *direct* the culture. From there, *building* culture is more of an art than a science. People need to be engaged from the bottom-up and engaged early."

I am continually astounded by how many companies keep culture change initiatives isolated at the top or believe they are doing a good deed by delegating the engagement or execution to a committee.

I am not surprised, though, when the same organizations complain that they are not making enough progress in improving their culture, because it has been an isolated journey.

If you have 50–100 employees, you should be able to engage and collect feedback from most of them. However, that is unrealistic for larger organizations. If an organization has 100,000 or even 2,000 employees, you may wonder how that is even possible. When I suggest that leaders should engage the organization on a deeper level, I don't mean that they should meet with every single employee. That would not only take an eternity, but the harsh reality is that there are probably a few employees in every organization who should not have a say in shaping the future culture.

Some employees only care about collecting a paycheck and doing just enough to get by so their manager doesn't notice their lackluster effort. This doesn't mean that leaders and people managers should automatically write these people off and not care or strive to develop them as time goes on, but their input should not shape the future of the organization.

A Collaborative, Multifaceted Approach

After selecting "Get Better Today. . .Together" as their cultural purpose statement (CPS), senior leaders at SGWS-IL began communicating it with their teams and divisions. They were now ready for the next stage of the process. This involved a collaborative, "hearts and minds," multifaceted approach to drive engagement and identify key daily behaviors that would help bring the values to life.

The collaborative, multifaceted approach consists of the four following areas:

1. **Identification:** Uncover and identify problem areas of the existing culture.
2. **Engagement:** Engage every manager in the company for their feedback and input.
3. **Transformation:** Turn values into clear and specific daily behaviors.

4. **Managerial Development:** Begin company-wide manager meetings.

To help you understand each of the four steps better, I'll summarize the main objectives and importance of each step.

Step #1: Identification: Identify Problem Areas of the Existing Culture

To change anything, including culture, an acute understanding of the current reality is needed. And this is not as simple as it sounds, because most leaders want to start driving change and running full-steam-ahead right away. The first step was to identify the current culture's negative pressure points and significant problem areas. We began with the senior leadership team at SGWS-IL. Even though we talked briefly about problem areas when choosing the cultural purpose statement, the goal this time was to dig much deeper and find the root causes.

While simultaneously conducting ongoing discussions with the senior leaders, we also looped in the managers. We not only wanted their input and to hear directly from them on what the biggest problems and challenges were from their point of view, but all people managers were encouraged to ask their direct reports the same thing. They would then report back during the next few meetings and share anonymously what their teams and direct reports shared with them.

Step #2: Engagement: Involve Every Manager in the Company

Following the discovery of several problem areas that had not been raised in earlier meetings or even prior employee engagement surveys at SGWS-IL, the next phase was to engage and involve every manager in the company in the planning process. Although all people managers were involved in the identification and examination of key problem areas, we wanted to involve them in a more intimate setting. These meetings were held with managers from each division of the company, with no senior executives present. Our goal was to make the managers feel enough at ease to share whatever was on their minds without fear of the leader they reported to being present.

I facilitated the group discussions with divisional managers. The primary goal was for them to share unique qualities and characteristics of the company in their own words, in addition to expanding on the problem areas that we had been discussing for months. It was critical to hear their perspectives on what made the company unique. This was an important part of the process to encourage collaboration and also be brutally honest. This engagement process ensured that every manager would play an important role in the culture from here on.

Step #3: Transformation: Turn Values into Specific Daily Behaviors

Following the meetings with divisional managers, the next step in the process was to concentrate on translating values into specific and repeated daily behaviors. Even though they had inspiring values, which they referred to as their FAMILY Values, those values were not translated into specific behaviors related to their organization and daily workload.

Over many months, we compiled and analyzed the feedback and submissions from each of my meetings with division managers. The goal was to not just create a behavior and assign it to each value. We wanted to pinpoint the daily behaviors that would not only enhance the health of the organization, but also enhance the business and drive commercial execution. This was of the utmost importance because that is the part of culture-building that commonly gets lost in translation. *To drive, transform, and support the business.* This part of the process was rigorous and consisted of many meetings going back and forth, being patient but also moving with great intention and urgency. It started with the senior leadership team analyzing where the business was, where it needed to go, and finally, discussing the behaviors that were crucial to support the values but also win in the marketplace.

After the senior leaders completed the first draft, every single manager in the company gave their feedback on each of the values and behaviors. The senior leaders and managers broke off into breakout groups to discuss the value that their group was assigned. Every group was asked to focus on the daily behaviors through the lens of the entire company and to think not only in terms of their division or their specific roles. We ended up collecting over 200 pages of insights, ideas, and suggestions from every manager in the company. From there, the senior leaders went back and forth with the managers to gradually narrow down the feedback between meetings.

Step #4: Managerial Development: Conduct Company-Wide Manager Meetings

To successfully drive and change the culture of an organization requires a strong commitment to training and developing front-line managers. Senior leaders play an important role in shaping the culture and setting the tone. However, the successful adoption and execution of front-line managers will be a key factor in the success or failure of the journey. That is why it is important to not only engage them early in the process, but also nurture and place a strong emphasis on their development along the way.

At SGWS-IL, what initially started out as quarterly meetings for all people managers soon evolved into other aspects of the process. We established a monthly meeting schedule where we could discuss the actions, deliverables, and commitment of all leaders and managers.

There were two strategic objectives for these meetings:

1. We wanted not only to inform, educate, and coach the managers on the importance of culture but also to address any

misconceptions, while focusing on how to win with our execution. The goal of these meetings was to share real-life examples of the cultural purpose statement to make it easier to understand, read and discuss case studies together that were relevant to where the company was, and get people excited.

2. We wanted to diligently strive toward becoming a more connected management team at SGWS-IL. At every meeting, there was some sort of teambuilding exercise where the hundreds of managers in the company could get to know their peers on a deeper, heart-and-mind level. This was so powerful that in one of the very first meetings, when team members were sharing about their personal lives, there was hardly a dry eye in the room. Managers discovered information about colleagues they saw and interacted with on a regular basis—that they were completely unaware of. That is the strength of the heart-and-mind connection and the collaborative approach. This is an example of how employees gradually begin to feel psychologically safe with one another.

While all the above actions were occurring on a regular basis, the cultural purpose statement (CPS) was still being communicated throughout the organization. It was important that leaders and managers incorporated the mantra, "Get Better Today. . .Together" in everything they did, but also to educate the rest of the organization on what to expect soon. On top of this, there was a deliberate focus on sharing the "why" behind everything that was happening. This can be problematic in many ways when the organization has never communicated, or apprised the others of *why* change is happening, *why* they should get on board, and *why* it's crucial for them to do so. This level of communication and collaboration creates a real sense of co-creation, rather than just being directed from the top down.

When senior leaders began to modify their actions and communication methods, that change spread to other departments, managers, and employees across the entire company. They felt safe and didn't fear punishment. As a result, everyone's heart and mind were opened, and the business set up a strong way of working together.

The leader of SGWS-IL's entire selling division, Mike Housey, and I had a meeting one day. He worked closely with other leaders to direct every facet of the cultural evolution. I asked him what the most significant difference was between the four-step process described earlier in this chapter and previous attempts.

"Since day one, it has been a completely game-changing experience," said Mike. He continued: "The unique part is that every single manager in the company has their fingerprints on the culture that we are building. It is not coming from just the senior leaders, and that has been transformational. I have always been inspired by our FAMILY Values and what they represent but distilling those values into clear behaviors related to us specifically here in Illinois has been incredible."

"Collaboration makes a difference." I smiled. It was remarkable to see the leaders come together and unite. I remembered Aristotle's quote, "The whole is better than the sum of its parts." I had witnessed this as early as my football days at Indiana with Coach Hep when he coined the mantra, "Get Better Today." And then later, SGWS-IL took that mantra and expanded it to: "Get Better Today. . .Together."

There is no doubt that Terry Brick, the head of SGWS-IL, did an excellent job of articulating the "why" behind all of his actions. Over a period of a few months, small changes began to accumulate and eventually become a routine practice. Even though SGWS-IL was already a high-performing organization, this level of detail and consistency devoted to leadership development and culture was a unique experience for nearly every leader in the company.

As a senior leadership team, we continued to meet on a regular basis to hold each other accountable and to have an open and frequent dialogue about what is working well, what needs to be changed, and how to continuously drive clarity and commitment in the next steps.

Driving Cultural Meaning and Impact

Building a superior, world-class culture cannot be rushed. It cannot consist of an annual executive retreat with a strictly top-down approach that is completed in a single weekend. Even establishing a set of core values and writing them down on banners or brochures and plastering them everywhere while constantly discussing them are not enough. Temporarily, it may gain some traction, but all talk and no action will not suffice.

The benefits of this collaborative approach have been nothing short of remarkable. There will always be challenges along the journey, but when fully committed to, the collaboration will cultivate meaning and impact. With a committed senior leadership team, working with all of the company's people managers can be a transformative experience and help bring much-needed energy to an initiative that usually drains energy and excitement more than it brings.

This approach can have a significant impact because not only do front-line and middle managers sometimes understand cultural challenges better than senior leaders, but they are also involved in their creation and development. This helps drive a deeper meaning, which is important because large-scale changes in culture or behavior will never happen without the alignment and commitment of management.

Another aspect of this process that is largely overlooked is the breakdown of silos and the formation of a healthier and more connected management team. There will be some resistance at the start of the process, and you should expect that there will never be complete buy-in from everyone. Over time, though, with consistency and prioritization of effort, bonds are formed, and the business impact can be amplified as a result of the habit of senior leaders and people managers discussing urgent and important matters.

No matter where you are on the culture journey, taking a more collaborative approach can pay huge dividends and do far more than just lay the groundwork for a better culture.

Action Plan for Leaders

Here is a plan of action to help you get started. Feel free to adapt this to your organization's needs and current situation.

1. **Uncover and identify problem areas of existing culture:**
   - Examine the current systems, processes, and organizational structure. What is working and what could use some tweaking? Are there any systems, processes, or organizational structures that are negatively affecting your culture? Speed? Overall impact?
   - Analyze and discuss previous employee engagement survey scores. Identify and be aware of prior pockets of growth and dissect what exactly has been done up to the current reality. Has it been working or what could be more effective?
   - Senior leaders and all people managers start asking direct reports and teams what they enjoy about the existing culture, what they would fix or enhance if they were leading the charge, and, in their opinion, what shifts would make the greatest impact.
   - Encourage all people managers to collect ideas and insights from their direct reports on what should change and what needs to change.
   - What is the ideal future state for your culture? What does that look like?

2. **Engage all people managers:**
   - Senior leaders should set up meetings and start engaging all people managers in the company. Depending on the size of the organization, this will most likely be done in separate breakout groups by division or function. Smaller companies should be able to have meetings as one cohesive group.
   - Communicate the importance of these meetings and reiterate to all managers that their role in building a better culture is pivotal.

- Collect feedback and insights from managers on how they view the company and what makes it unique and special to them.
- Identify the key mindsets and behavioral shifts that are required to build not only a better workplace, but also a culture that drives business execution.
- What root-causes of cultural tension and barriers do we need to be aware of?

3. **Turn values into clear and specific daily behaviors:**

- Clearly communicate that the values *not lived* are just as effective as not having a set of values at all. Remind everyone that values alone do not build culture. Culture is built and determined by behavior at scale. Repeated behaviors, day in and day out.
- Senior leaders and all people managers should assess how well the organization has lived up to the values of the company.
- Does your current set of values excite and energize everyone in the company? Spend some time revisiting them. Do they need changing at all?
- Are there specific daily behaviors for each of the values where employees know exactly what is expected of them?
- Given the current landscape of your business and the market, what key behaviors are crucial to win and keep up with the rapidly changing conditions?
- Senior leaders and people managers must collaborate on identifying daily behaviors for each of the values. Ensure that the behaviors tied to the values are concise and relatable across the entire organization.

4. **Begin company-wide manager meetings:**

- Depending on your current training and meeting schedule, start quarterly or monthly company-wide manager meetings.

- Utilize these meetings as an opportunity to drive a deeper connection and build more trust between senior leaders and people managers.

- Perform teambuilding exercises, share best practices, and have participants discuss real-time challenges and insights as it relates to the current business and culture journey.

- Spend an adequate amount of time coaching and teaching on the importance of culture. Share best practices and effective techniques on how managers can build culture, communicate the culture, and drive collaboration and culture expectations. Make it a habit to talk about culture and breaking down silos.

- Understand that the purpose of these meetings is to become a more connected and cohesive management team while actively co-creating the culture.

CHAPTER 8

The Culture Implementation Playbook

Culture does not change because we desire to change it. Culture changes when the organization is transformed; the culture reflects the realities of people working together every day.

—Frances Hasselbein, former CEO of Girl Scouts of the USA

"Hi, Matt. Thank you for your talk today. Would you mind signing your book for me?" The young lady looked like she was in her late thirties or early forties, with shoulder-length brown hair, wearing a casual jacket with slacks. By all appearances, she was professional and driven, and yet she frowned, as if something was bothering her.

"Sure, I'll be happy to sign it. Did you enjoy my talk?" I smiled big, expecting to hear a few takeaways she got from my talk.

"Mmm . . . uh . . . sure." She flipped her hair back off her shoulders and half-smiled. But her brows were furrowed, and I wondered if something was wrong. *Maybe I missed the mark with my talk.*

Pen in hand, I fidgeted behind a table piled high with a stack of my books, *Winning Plays: Tackling Adversity and Achieving Success in Business and Life,* published in 2016.

I had been standing there for a solid 20 minutes, greeting people who had attended my keynote at a large convention, comprised of several different Fortune 500 leaders. A good part of my talk was focused on how sports and leaders in business are similar when it comes to building culture, and how leaders could excel if they incorporated a playbook like sports coaches do.

"Uh . . . so, you didn't like my talk?" I asked lightheartedly. I needed to know if I had offended her or missed the mark somehow but still keep the conversation light.

"No, no, nothing like that," she said. She handed me her copy of my book.

I sighed deeply. *You never know what people are dealing with and it isn't always about you,* I told myself.

"Alright, then, who should I make it out to?" I asked, deciding to just avoid the topic of my talk.

"Angela."

"O.K., Angela. Which company are you with?" I took her copy of *Winning Plays* and opened it to the title page.

"I just got a promotion to Executive Vice President for a utilities company and what you said hit home."

"Congratulations!" Encouraged, I added, "I hope you learned something useful today to help you in your new role."

"Your talk was great. Truly. I was so moved. But to tell you the truth, I don't have a clue what I'm doing. The person who was supposed to get the job suddenly died of a heart attack and I was next in line, though I don't feel like I'm qualified or ready. I'm worried and when you started talking about sports coaches and their detailed playbooks, and all this culture change rhetoric, I had to wonder if I was going to get lost and drown in this position. I don't have a playbook or let alone one page on how to build culture. Or what I should do. Neither does the company. I mean, I love sports and business, both, I really do . . . but . . ."

"Look, I'm sure you're more ready than you realize and have great potential," I said. "They wouldn't have promoted you if they didn't believe in you."

She shrugged her shoulders.

I bent over, wrote a note of good luck and best wishes to Angela, then signed my name.

I briefly watched Angela take her book and walk toward the exit. I then turned to the next person in line.

Angela isn't alone in her confusion. Many business leaders around the world have recognized the need or desire to improve their organization's culture, and many still wonder, "What is this?" or "How do I exactly go about doing this?"

Using specific terms and protocols that all leaders are familiar with has been extremely helpful to me in my work with organizations over the years in terms of building culture. To describe how to implement a culture change in an organization, I use the football-specific term "playbook." A cultural playbook for your company, even if you aren't a sports fan or know a lot about football, is still extremely beneficial. Even if you don't want to change your company's culture completely, you still need a good playbook outlining the best ways to plan, execute, and win. I will discuss this more later in this chapter.

Imagine This Scenario

An organization has decided on and appointed a new set of core values. Every leader who has seen a version of the new values has agreed with them and thought they were spot on. The senior leadership team has met with each department in the company several times to get their ideas and gauge how their employees feel.

The extensive and often stressful discussions about the impending cultural change have finally concluded. This has been an agonizing but equally exhilarating experience for the leaders of this organization.

It's finally time to launch the new and improved strategy for their culture to the rest of the organization, after all the blood, sweat, and tears that have gone into improving the culture. The leaders are nervous, proud, and excited, and their minds are running through every possible outcome in their heads.

The management team was eager to accelerate the process and communicate the new company culture. They believed that the difficult work had already been completed, and that the most important thing at this point was to simply share the fruits of their labor and figure out the rest.

The long-awaited day finally arrived. The new culture was rolled out to the rest of the company. The CEO of the company gave a heavily scripted speech, which was far from an authentic and inspiring introduction to the new culture. In the coming weeks, each of the 10,000 employees would receive a fifty-slide PowerPoint deck, as well as an email from the leadership team explaining the change in more detail. New posters had been hung throughout the company's headquarters, and inspirational tag lines had been painted on the walls.

However, no core communication strategy was in place, resulting in leaders and managers sending mixed messages. Not only that, but some leaders felt compelled to and comfortable talking about culture, while others felt the opposite.

The energy was high in the beginning, and the anticipation of a brighter, bigger future seemed to grow with each passing moment. That started to quickly change, though. With the passage of time, the company's challenges and demands grew as well. A year earlier, a competitor had entered the market who posed no real threat at the time. However, that same competitor recently merged with a $100 billion tech company that was innovative and bold and was sure to make some noise in the months ahead. Not to mention that, with all the internal and external change that seemed to be happening at the same time, the organization's overall morale was beginning to suffer.

The enthusiasm and excitement for the new culture faded and lost all momentum in what seemed like the blink of an eye. Even though most leaders thought there was a decent plan in place to launch their organizational culture and finally build it to take them to the top, the reality was that they had no concrete plan.

Yes, they had a new set of core values, a PowerPoint pitch deck, and had held a few meetings before launching their culture. Their error was in believing that once it was shared with the organization, everything would fall into place.

The CEO delivered a scripted speech that did everything but inspire everyone for the culture they were about to co-create together. Because of this, the results were minimal due to their inability to formulate a plan for implementation and the excitement they wanted to generate with their culture.

There may have been some positive outcomes that first day, but only because so many long-serving employees were desperate for a change of culture. The unfortunate aspect of this scenario is not the failure to successfully launch and implement the new culture, but rather the wasted time and energy leading up to that day and continuing afterwards.

You may or may not have followed a similar path when trying to improve or change your organization's culture, but many leaders and managers have. In the early stages, there is usually a lot of energy built up for the rollout, and it may even gain fast momentum, with leaders thinking the new or revamped culture is a success.

However, as time passes and the pace of business accelerates, the momentum and excitement fade just as quickly as the pent-up demand and energy at the start of the process.

As each day comes to an end and a new day begins, the priority of focusing on and building culture is pushed aside in favor of everything else. At the end of the year, the leadership team gathers for their end-of-the-year review meeting and says to one another, "At least we tried."

This was a similar situation to the experience I had working with a large company in the auto industry for the past two years. Over the previous six years, the company had gone through a lot of transformation. They were losing a lot of top talent due to management dysfunction, and they had just completed a digital transformation that altered deep-rooted processes and systems in a variety of ways that employees had been used to working for two decades.

I met Jason, who was the Chief Operating Officer at the time, at a major conference I spoke at a few years ago in Orlando, Florida. We kept in touch every now and then, but the timing was never right to start working together. When the digital transformation happened, the rapid change started to consume and control the organization, rather than the *organization* leading and directing the change.

Jason contacted me, and we eventually agreed on a time for me to visit the company's headquarters and meet with the management team for a half-day.

It was a bright and early Tuesday morning when I walked into the boardroom. I'll never forget the look of despair on every leader's face that morning. Several were yawning, and several were perusing stacks of paper in front of them.

It was so early that the rest of the employees hadn't even arrived at work yet.

The meeting began with everyone pouring a cup of coffee. There was the usual smalltalk and catching up.

I sat next to Jason, and we talked quietly about the weather and my flight while people finished pouring coffee.

"Good morning, everyone, and thank you for coming in early for this meeting," Jason said after everyone settled down. "I'd like you to meet Matt Mayberry, a leadership and culture consultant, who's going to help us with some ideas for implementing a playbook for our culture change."

"Good morning." I nodded and smiled. "I'm happy to be here."

"Why don't all of you briefly introduce yourselves?" Jason suggested.

One by one, everyone briefly said their names and positions around the conference table.

"My name is Marc, I'm the Senior Vice President of Operations, but I don't believe there is much value in me sharing more about myself. What I really want to speak about is how much I absolutely love this company. I've been here for twenty-one years, and if I have my way, I'll be here for the rest of my working life. I'm passionate about the people who will soon flood the halls of this company around nine a.m. I admire them, and they deserve better because of my love and admiration for this company. Even before the internal transformation we just underwent, our culture was a top priority, but all attempts to change it have failed." Marc paused to take a sip of his coffee before continuing, "I feel like we do a good job all the way up to the point where it's time to implement and drive the change we want to see in the rest of the company. Everything seems to fall out of place from there."

I had already witnessed all of this. Companies initiate cultural change with a bang and excitement by employing grand ideas. Then, as time passes, they simply fizzle out and their initial efforts wither away because they lack a comprehensive cultural playbook for launching, embedding, and cascading their culture.

Common Culture Implementation Pain Points

The frustration expressed by the auto company in implementing and launching a culture change at scale is not uncommon. I've seen businesses that get almost everything right from the start. They are committed to bringing about organizational change and improving the working environment for their employees.

They set aside time and prioritize their calendars to ensure that they have the difficult conversations that are necessary for things to change. They even include multiple groups of employees to ensure that the employee voice is heard at all levels of the organization.

However, when the time comes to finally launch and implement their culture, the momentum and overall organizational impact are significantly reduced. Even if there are some early wins in the beginning, the likelihood of continuing those early wins diminishes over time.

Why is this?

Even if an organization's entire leadership team and every single employee recognize the need for a culture shift, how is this possible?

How can this be when hours upon hours are spent planning the future and deciding what changes will occur along the way?

There could be a variety of reasons for this, and what is true for one company may be the exact opposite for another.

With that in mind, let's look at some of the common pain points I've seen over the years that limit the impact of a company implementing and cascading culture change at scale on an ongoing basis.

Six Implementation Pain Points

1. **Poor preparation and planning:** Some organizations spend a lot of time thinking about how to change and improve their culture, but much less time developing a playbook for relentlessly implementing and cascading the procedures required for this change to take root. This can lead to a chaotic and disorganized effort. Even if you are only improving certain aspects of your existing culture rather than undergoing a complete transformation, you still need a playbook. The plan for how the culture will be communicated, the length of the rollout phase, and the early wins that the company will strive for must be highlighted in this playbook. Excellence in culture implementation begins with a strong commitment to preparation and planning.

2. **Lack of understanding and relatability:** If there is a lack of understanding of the culture, it becomes nearly impossible to make it relatable for the organization and clearly show how every employee plays a role in the desired change. Let's say a few senior leaders agree to change the culture but aren't clear on what the new culture should be. Do you think those leaders will be effective in communicating the new culture to their team members and the organization? Obviously not. Only 27% of U.S. employees, according to Gallup, believe in their company's values.[1] There must be a deep understanding of the culture and why the change or shift is happening. The clearer the understanding, the more relatable the message will be for most employees.

3. **Misrepresentation of old mindsets and behaviors:** Changing culture at scale is more complicated than simply *communicating* in a weekly meeting the new procedures and behaviors that leaders urge everyone in the organization to adopt. Changing a mindset or behavior requires much more than motivation. To start driving the organization in a completely different direction, everyone in the organization must be fully aware of the old ways of working and why they are no longer helpful for the future. Sharing a revised list of your core values and communicating the new vision and direction for your culture will only do so much. People need to understand what they are abandoning and how the new ways of working will help them both personally and professionally.

4. **Insufficient communication strategy:** Assuming that you can drive culture change at scale by communicating your desired outcome in the same way you communicate everything else is a recipe for mediocrity. I've seen leaders hold a single company-wide meeting with all 10,000 of their employees, believing that the one meeting will be enough to bring about the desired change. Other leaders, believe it or not, have relied on sending a series of emails to the entire company in the hopes of changing deeply ingrained

mindsets and behaviors. Today, people are bombarded every day in their email inboxes. The communication of your culture alone will not result in long-term change, but to successfully implement culture change throughout an organization, communicating it as you do for everything else will not cut it.

5. **Absence of shared behavioral shifts:** As I have previously said, values alone do not create and build culture. Living your values only some of the time does not contribute to the creation and maintenance of culture. Changing values into behaviors is only half the battle. Certainly, this is a step in the right direction, but those behaviors must then be shared and distributed widely throughout the organization, along with a clear and concise description of what is expected. It is not enough to simply talk about it. It is critical to have a visual representation of the specific behaviors that leaders and all people managers can use to coach their people. Just like a sports team has a playbook with specific plays designed to help them perform well and win, your company should have a playbook with the key shifts needed to transform your culture into action and turn your values into winning behaviors.

6. **Failing to highlight positive examples:** Not highlighting and sharing early wins is detrimental to building momentum during any change program and generating positive energy during any change program is non-negotiable. It can be exhausting and frustrating to ask people, especially a large group of people, to change aspects of their current way of working. There will be reservations, a great deal of uncertainty, and even some harsh negativity. Making a concerted effort to highlight early successes and share examples with the rest of the organization can help to set a strong tone for the future. When highlighting positive examples, it is also important to call out and coach those who are not setting a good example.

A Playbook for Driving Transformation at Scale

When I played football at Indiana University and later for the Chicago Bears, each player was given a detailed playbook at the start of training camp. These playbooks were well over 100 pages long and were kept in a heavy binder. These were our ground rules. Our guides. Our Bibles. They included everything from a descriptive list of defensive or offensive plays depending on which side of the ball you were on, to detailed statistics, team goals and objectives, and cultural guidelines. We carried these playbooks with us wherever we went.

A playbook in sports is much more than just sketches and diagrams of the coach's designed plays. Instead, it tells the entire story of how a team builds a scheme or plan from the ground up by utilizing a "together" strategy involving all units and players.

Don't forget: When it comes to launching and implementing culture, we as leaders need our own playbook.

Now that we've identified the common challenges of launching and implementing a culture change, it's time to focus our efforts on driving transformation at scale.

The early stages of launching and introducing a culture shift or change to the rest of a company are critical because if there is a lack of traction from the start, gaining momentum and recovering from that point forward will be extremely difficult.

After nearly a year and a half of hard work with Southern Glazer's Wine and Spirits of Illinois (SGWS-IL), we were finally ready to launch the culture. What was unique about arriving at this point in introducing the culture to the rest of the company was seeing the progress that had already been made. Even from just communicating the "Get Better Today . . . Together" cultural purpose statement and watching the different approaches in how team members were communicating with one another was special to witness.

Change didn't happen overnight. It required arduous effort, which was initially met with aggressive opposition, so the change took root gradually. Finally, other division leaders began to see a glimmer of hope that their hard work was paying off, even if only in a small way. Encouraged, the desire to take it to the next level grew.

Because our world is continuously evolving, there is always a higher level to go. One more step. Even though a great deal of effort and planning goes into communicating and launching the culture, the process does not end there. It's tempting to believe that once the culture has been shared and communicated with the organization, we can relax and take our foot off the pedal. It is critical to establish the precedent during every meeting that there is more work to be done to improve and get better. Always.

If you want to successfully implement and drive culture change at scale, you must shock the organization. When I tell you to shock the organization, I am not referring to negative connotations. Simply put, you must convey a moving and compelling message that sends shockwaves throughout the company. There must be vigor and enthusiasm in the delivery. It must be purposeful, so everyone can envision what the future vision will look like. There needs to be numerous and diverse channels of communication cascading throughout the organization, and the delivery needs to be consistent and continuous. This may come across as a little overbearing or aggressive, but changing or improving an organization's culture is not a soft undertaking. To avoid joining the long list of companies that have failed to implement change initiatives, it is necessary to do things differently and with far more tenacity and focus than others.

Culture Implementation Playbook

Here is a breakdown of the SGWS-IL culture implementation playbook we crafted, paying close attention to the pain points I mentioned earlier. Four actions were included in the cultural implementation playbook.

Action#1: Drive Alignment Forward

I worked closely with the leadership team, and before we did anything, we made sure that every leader and manager in the company were all on the same page. We used the meetings we had already scheduled to summarize all the earlier feedback sessions, the desired impact we wanted to achieve, and the overarching message we wanted to convey to the entire organization.

These meetings were important because, although we had already discussed extensively how we wanted to launch the culture, we needed to be certain that everyone understood the key priorities. The impact would never be what we wanted it to be without complete alignment, understanding, and care concerning what we were trying to carry out.

The planning and preparation meetings were communicative and collaborative. There were no wasted movements. No wasted energy. Our goal was to gather input from managers at all levels regarding what they thought would have the greatest impact.

After a few meetings with senior leaders and managers, and once there was alignment, we decided on an official date for Terry Brick to unveil the revamped culture.

Action #2: Behavioral Manifesto

The Behavioral Manifesto included clear and concise behavioral statements for each of the cultural pillars. These were made up of seven behaviors that were decided upon during the collaborative meetings mentioned in the earlier chapter. The behavioral manifesto was a one-page master document that would be referenced, shared, and integrated into nearly everything that came after. It would be a constant reminder of the behaviors that would help bring the cultural purpose statement "Get Better Today . . . Together" to life. These were behavioral norms to fulfill and support the SGWS FAMILY Values.

Even though this may appear to be just a document—skeptics will be quick to point out that a great culture isn't built on a document—the Behavioral Manifesto ended up being a complete gamechanger. As I have stated many times throughout this book, a single document will not magically transform culture and perform miracles. However, this Behavioral Manifesto did provide clarity around the daily behaviors and mindsets needed to win. The most important thing was to "walk the talk," but shifting the focus from values to repeated daily behaviors was a step in the right direction.

Action#3: Communication Strategy

While communicating your culture does not, in and of itself, *build* anything, it is critical in the early stages of any change initiative to develop a thorough and strategic communication gameplan. If you don't communicate the culture in an inspiring and powerfully captivating way, utilizing an engaging "hearts and minds" approach, you'll make the job of driving it forward even more difficult. This does not imply that leaders should change their personalities or communication styles on a regular basis, but it does imply that more effort is needed than simply putting together a PowerPoint deck or sending out a company email.

After creating the Behavioral Manifesto for SGWS-IL, we outlined an extensive communication strategy. This focused on the following points of emphasis that helped guide the creation of every speech and discussion of launching and implementing the culture.

- **Reality:** The current reality of where SGWS-IL was as an organization.
- **Why:** A detailed breakdown of why this change is happening and why it's important.
- **What:** An outline of the expectations moving forward and how these affected everyone.
- **Meaning:** How does this help the organization, the core mission, and every individual?
- **Vision:** Establish a clear and compelling vision of the future for SGWS-IL.

- **Business impact:** Highlight the business impact and how suppliers and customers would be benefited.
- **Togetherness:** Emphasize the difference we can make in our communities and with one another by working together as one unit and living the cultural purpose statement, "Get Better Today . . . Together."

Action #4: Culture Rollout Roadmap

We then created a roadmap for the cultural rollout. The purpose of the roadmap was to outline every phase of the launch journey for clarity, accountability, and maximum impact. The roadmap consisted of three phases:

Phase 1: Communication

- At a company-wide meeting, Terry Brick would introduce the "Get Better Today . . . Together" (GBTT) culture.
- Every vice president in the company would hold meetings with their teams to explain how the GBTT culture related to their particular divisions and daily work protocols.
- All managers would coach their teams on the meaning behind GBTT and connect how daily behaviors apply to everyone's current role.
- Division directors and frontline managers would meet with direct reports to drive an even deeper meaning behind the GBTT culture.

Phase 2: Embed

- A physical copy of the GBTT Behavioral Manifesto would be given to every employee.
- A recognition program for employees would be started for those who embraced and lived the GBTT culture.
- Daily emphasis would be placed on behavioral communication and mindset adjustments.

- Leaders and managers would integrate new methods and best practices into the current structures and processes of the organization.

Phase 3: Engage

- Key team members would be identified and utilized by leaders and managers.
- Culture town hall meetings and roadshows were to be held on a regular basis.
- Employees would share best practices and key initiatives.
- Dissecting cultural imperatives in an ongoing cultural committee meeting.

Phase 1: Communication   The first phase of the culture roll-out roadmap was to make sure not only that the culture was communicated, but that the message was also driven deep into the organization. When a company has over 1,000 employees, it is critical to have multiple touchpoints rather than just one companywide meeting where a leader speaks from a scripted Power-Point deck.

Even if a company has fewer than a thousand employees, it is critical to embrace all forms of communication, including regular meetings, newsletters, and gatherings with different departments within the company.

Our goal was to have Terry Brick kick off the culture's launch and share how it would help bring the SGWS-IL FAMILY Values to life. Once that happened, every VP, leader, and all people managers in the company would meet with their divisions and teams to discuss how to make the culture relevant to their specific daily functions.

It's worth noting that these meetings were more than just leaders and managers discussing culture with their teams. These were meetings focused on two-way communication, with time set aside at the end of each meeting for team members to showcase their ideas and feedback on how their division could implement these changes. The communication phase lasted approximately six weeks. An important tool in our effort to improve communication was a checklist that leaders and managers could use as a reference point as the journey continued. As an example, here's a sample of the communication checklist:

- Am I constantly emphasizing the importance of "Get Better Today . . . Together" and the purpose of the culture we want to create?
- Am I coaching team members and reinforcing the Behavioral Manifesto?
- Have I clearly articulated the purpose, priorities, and cultural expectations?
- Am I consistently establishing a personal connection with my team members and expressing how they fit into the big picture?
- Are my team members' concerns and suggestions being heard, and am I acting on this information as it comes to my attention?
- No matter what I say, do my actions reflect what I expect of others?

Phase 2: Embed The second phase focused on embedding the GBTT culture. Every employee received a copy of the GBTT Behavioral Manifesto, and each month, employees who demonstrated the behaviors were publicly recognized. These were everyday examples of employees going above and beyond for a supplier or customer, or even doing something to support another team member.

All leaders and managers were asked to submit the name of anyone they saw who clearly exemplified one of the cultural pillars. The selected individuals were not simply mentioned. The example of what they did was shared with the rest of the company to emphasize the behavior and set the standard for everyone else.

The GBTT Behavioral Manifesto was embedded in internal meetings and training sessions. There was constant discussion about whether the behaviors were being adhered to and what could be done differently to generate an even greater impact.

It's one thing to regularly communicate and talk about your culture, but unless it's deeply ingrained in your employees and your company, the results will be minimal. Even though this was a dedicated phase during the rollout, proper cultural embedding is a never-ending process. This was something that would be ongoing and consistent.

In the embed phase, the non-negotiables are:

- Provide unrelenting focus on the behaviors associated with each core value and the explanation of how they can be cultivated and lived day-to-day.
- Describe and explain the positive impact on both the individual and the business of doing things differently.

Phase 3: Engaging Engaging the entire organization was the target of the third phase. This phase, like the others, is ongoing and will eventually be fully integrated into the long-term, driving sustainability strategy. Nonetheless, this was a crucial aspect of the rollout phase in terms of fostering culture change and transformation at scale. It was important to find and engage respected, high-potential employees in the company who were not senior leaders or middle managers.

These individuals were a key part of taking the message to the next level and helping distribute the desired changes. Every senior leader and manager was encouraged to gather feedback on how to best support team members on a regular basis to decide what was working well and what was not.

Regular active listening sessions were held to listen to the organization. It was important to listen to what employees had to say and to acknowledge how they felt. This was the way to learn what they thought leaders and managers could do better to support and help them in the pursuit of "Get Better

Today . . . Together." Obviously, not every idea that was brought up in these meetings could be put into action, but these active listening sessions were very helpful and continue to this day to be a great way to find and remedy potential problems.

Moving with Urgency and Adaptability

It wasn't long after the SGWS-IL culture was launched and widely disseminated that the organization was buzzing with excitement and enthusiasm. It felt like a huge weight had been lifted off the shoulders of every leader, despite the fact that there was still much work to be done and that this was only the beginning of a never-ending journey.

It took feverishly hard work to get to this point. Many leaders found the process extremely rewarding, and it was especially satisfying for them to personally witness the company's radical transformation from where it had been just a few years ago. No longer did they have a set of values that were only discussed on a few occasions throughout the year. In order to live out their values in everything they did, they had a well-defined culture with clear and concise behavioral shifts that they aspired to live out every day.

By making their communication and actions more inclusive, leaders were gradually shifting away from a command-and-control management style. Silos remained, but they were shrinking month by month as leaders and managers made a conscious effort to do so. The most important thing was having a clear game plan and strategy for how to move forward.

Did everything go as planned? Quite the contrary. There is no such thing as perfection in building culture, or anything else for that matter. You and everyone else will be caught off guard by obstacles that are nearly impossible to foresee. For example, SGWS-IL wasn't expecting to face government restrictions and a global pandemic in 2020 when they were launching and implementing their culture. The good news is that most of the work on their GBTT culture had already been completed before the crisis. However, due to the constraints and realities of the time, nimble leadership and adaptability were necessary.

The GBTT culture rollout was a success thanks to Terry Brick's outstanding leadership and the efforts of every other leader and manager in the organization. Hundreds of examples from employees at all levels exemplified what "Get Better Today . . . Together" was about.

Unforeseen circumstances provided an opportunity to delay or reschedule the entire culture rollout. As a result of the team's unwavering commitment to changing the culture and its extensive leadership development efforts, there was no going back. A detailed playbook of the journey ahead ensured that the vision never faded for SGWS-IL, encouraging them to stay committed to the ongoing strategies.

I recently gave a presentation on leadership in front of a group of 500 pharmaceutical industry executives. My message was about leading through change and building a winning culture. Jeffrey, one of the company's top executives, invited me to a private lunch after I gave my talk.

We had a light lunch, and then, just as we were about to get up from the table so I could head to the airport to go home, Jeffrey asked me, "Matt, what decides maximum impact versus minimal impact after leaders communicate a culture change?"

"Moving with a strong sense of urgency and adaptability," I replied.

Moving with urgency helps to generate traction and momentum for the plan for your culture that has been developed, implemented, and cascaded by the organization's leaders.

That is why, when it comes time for the rollout of your culture, you should conduct meetings and take part in the difficult and sometimes strenuous work of listening to others, gathering feedback, and thinking long and hard about the message you want to deliver. Only then will you be able to move quickly and with a strong sense of urgency. And, even if you have a detailed plan in place for your cultural launch, unforeseen circumstances can put your ability to keep moving forward to the test. Staying committed to the plan and leading with adaptability ensure that your vision and tenacity in pursuit of excellence will never waver, no matter what unexpected turns you encounter.

Regardless of whether you're trying to completely transform your culture, shift specific aspects, or simply improve your culture from good to great, you need a playbook. Leaders who try to wing it or delegate it to someone else are doomed to fail. Changing your company's culture for the better must have a strong first impression on your employees.

Culture Implementation Playbook Action Steps

You will need a well-prepared playbook to effectively introduce the culture change in your organization during the implementation phase of the journey. Every organization will have its own set of unique opportunities for making the most impact possible. During this stage of the process, everyone in the company will be introduced to your new or revamped culture. It's a great chance to get people excited about the changes and lay the groundwork for the future.

For a successful culture launch, let's put this phase into action by creating a playbook for culture implementation.

1. **Ensure management team alignment:** Prior to designing your culture implementation playbook, focus on ensuring management team alignment. Senior leaders and all people managers who will play a major role in launching and implementing the culture must be completely on board. Spend the time, no matter how many meetings it takes, making sure everyone understands the end goal and who will be doing what and when.

2. **Determine your official launch date:** After you've reached alignment with the management team, decide on your official

launch date. If at all possible, the date should be one that everyone in the organization can attend. For very large organizations, this could mean that a few hundred employees gather in person while everyone else watches via livestream. If operations are going to be put on hold for a while, it is almost certain that every division and function in the company will need to help with this.

3. **Craft your communication strategy:** Create your communication strategy and the overarching message you want to send to your organization and announce it in the kickoff meeting. Do not overlook this part. This should be done as a collective effort. Enlist your senior team and managers in the crafting of your message as the senior leader delivering the first kickoff message. It's critical that this message be genuine and authentic rather than heavily scripted. After you've finished your outline and written your speech, it's a good idea to practice in front of your team and make any necessary changes. How can you infuse as much energy as possible into explaining the deeper meaning of your culture and how you arrived at this point? Welcome their feedback and ask for suggestions.

4. **Plan how you will embed and cascade the launch:** After the kickoff meeting in which the senior leader launched the culture, what will be your process for embedding and cascading the message across the company? Depending on the size of the organization, this could take weeks or even months. As time goes on, there will undoubtedly be continuous and never-ending communication about the culture, but for the launch, it's best to leave nothing to chance. Every company leader and manager should not only have team meetings to spread the message, but they should also revisit it during one-on-one meetings and performance reviews shortly after the launch.

5. **Create your Behavioral Manifesto:** Call it whatever you want, but the most important thing is to create a concise document that converts your core values into clear daily behaviors

and into the overall team playbook. Make sure it's intended for the entire company and that it can be applied and translated to any role or responsibility. Managers can then relate it to the various divisions within the company.

6. **Take inventory on a regular basis:** Once your culture has been shared and communicated throughout the organization, keep track of what's working well and what might need to be tweaked, and then actively listen and adjust as needed. There will almost certainly be a few actions that have had an exponentially greater impact than everything else. Find out what those actions are and continue to perform them. If certain aspects of your original playbook aren't making a difference, don't be afraid to veer away from them. Inquire about feedback. Pay attention to people's body language as you walk through the halls. Every team meeting should begin with a pulse check.

7. **Share the plan:** Once you've finished your playbook, share it with others so they know exactly what to expect in the future. There will be more commitment from employees and a true sense that this is a team effort if every step in the journey forward is fully transparent.

8. **A word to the wise for frontline managers:** While senior leaders and the executive team have a lot of sway when it comes to changing culture, don't underestimate your ability to influence change as a frontline manager. You may see or hear things that even the most senior leaders are completely unaware of. The ability to create a healthier work environment and build a better culture is decided just as much by how well you model the culture as it is by senior leaders. Even if you don't think it matters, your actions most certainly do.

CHAPTER 9

Be Fanatical About Sustained Impact

A strong sustainability culture exists if people share a belief in sustainability's importance and behave in ways that support it.

—Edgar Schein, MIT Management Professor

*F*anatical is defined in this book in a way that may be similar to other definitions you'll find online: as having and being driven by an extreme and often unquestioning enthusiasm, devotion, obsession, or zeal for something. And for you, as a leader, that something needs to be culture. It is the air that organizations and leaders need to breathe. It is the food that they eat. The dreams of their sleep today and tomorrow. Being fanatical is an absolute must if you want to create a high-performing and thriving culture that will last.

With the right amount of determination, guidance, and initial burst of inspiration, anyone can get started on something they are extremely passionate about. Whether it's regaining control of your health, breaking a bad habit, or implementing a new process that has been put off for years in your organization, getting started isn't the real challenge. The real challenge is to be consistent, to continue pushing even when you don't want to, and to make it part of your everyday life.

This isn't to say that getting started isn't difficult or incredibly hard at times, but achieving excellence isn't completely reliant on getting started. If it were, every organization with a strong desire to build a better culture, improve employee engagement, or become more successful than they are today would do so.

At the end of each year, I choose one word as a theme for the following year. This one word serves as a guiding light in my life, reminding me of my dreams, goals, and aspirations for the coming year. Every aspect of my life is centered around this word. When life gets tough, it reminds me of what's most important and ignites a fire inside me when I'm feeling down. This exercise was introduced to me by Jon Gordon, a friend and bestselling author. Jon and his co-authors Dan Britton and Jimmy Page wrote the book, *One Word That Will Change Your Life*.[1]

The book focuses on the power of choosing one word to stand for a theme in your life for the coming year. Setting goals is important, but when we are going through difficult times and experiencing setbacks, reviewing our goals can make us feel even more stressed if we think that we aren't making progress.

On the other hand, choosing one word and keeping it front and center in our daily lives can provide tremendous clarity and keep us focused.

My one word for this year is *process*, which is why I'm sharing this particular exercise with you. For most of my life, I've been a goal-oriented person, always searching for the next target or objective to hit. I decided on *process* as my one word because I wanted to emphasize a much stronger focus on the process rather than the result.

When it comes to driving long-term cultural change and impact, ultimately, it all boils down to being *fanatical about the process* rather than the *outcome*, and the journey rather than the destination. In an organizational setting, once the vision is established and a solid foundation is in place, the difference between organizations that create cultural success and those that don't is based on their commitment to be consistent and focused on the ongoing process.

It does not matter how well your company has performed over the past five years or how great your company's culture has been in the past. Creating a sustainable culture that has an extraordinary impact on transforming business performance demands a special kind of love affair with what your organization does daily. *It demands unwavering fanaticism to the ongoing process and journey.*

During my conversation with Garry Ridge, Chairman and CEO of the WD-40 Company, he shared a quote from Larry Senn that perfectly captures the essence of this chapter: "Culture is not an initiative. All initiatives are enabled by culture."

Those words have a deeper meaning if you think about it. In a variety of ways, building culture or completely changing a company's culture may be viewed by some leaders as a separate initiative, and, partly, it is. In sections of this book, I use the term "initiative" to refer to cultural change.

However, viewing culture in its entirety as merely another initiative to check off a list is dangerous and can severely stifle any chance of achieving sustainable and long-term cultural success. So, a leadership team may call the process of improving and changing the current workplace culture an initiative. However, once that culture has been shared, it must be used as the basis for all aspects of the business.

I asked Garry why he believes many leaders struggle to create a culture that drives long-term organizational impact across the board. "A lack of consistency," he said. "Their culture is not deeply integrated into the business and is viewed as a separate function."

What he is really saying is that leaders aren't fanatical about the ongoing process of building culture.

Before we discuss how you can be fanatical about incorporating your culture into your day-to-day processes to ensure a lasting impact on the business, there are a few things to consider:

- **Culture fanaticism must be part of your DNA:** It is at this point in the process that the winners and losers are decided. Most leaders and organizations will try to build a better culture, but oftentimes, their efforts will eventually come to a halt. The damage and consequences end up being the same whether it's a month later, a year later, or even three years later. Remind yourself, all other leaders, managers, and every team member on a regular basis that launching your culture was maybe an initiative at first, but it is now a core part of who you are as an organization. Being fanatical with the processes that make up your company's culture is now a part of your DNA, something you live, breathe, sleep, and do every day.

- **Persist in your process:** As with every other stage of the culture-building process, you will meet ongoing resistance and challenges along the way, and you might be tempted to revert to old habits. Don't give in and fall prey to the trap. Avoid this at all costs. You might not get the results you are looking for right away, but be fanatical about hammering away at the process. Slowly but steadily, the tide will begin to turn in your favor. The real benefit of being fanatical and process-oriented is that each new day represents a new opportunity to turn things around and keep improving.

- **Keep a fanatical focus on impact areas:** Don't overburden yourself. Attempting to do too many things at once will backfire and produce the opposite result. There will be many ideas and insights shared as we progress through this chapter. Don't make things more difficult than they need to be. Find where you can have the most impact in your organization and begin there. Find where you can have the most impact in your day-to-day organizational processes, be fanatical about them, and begin there.

Framework for Driving Culture Sustainability

There is no such thing as a guarantee when it comes to maintaining a sustained, impactful culture. Having a great culture in the past does not guarantee that it will continue to be so in the future. However, a mediocre culture in a previous era does not guarantee a mediocre culture in the future. Even with the help of defining your culture, engaging the hearts and minds of the organization, and developing a solid playbook and roadmap to launch and embed your culture, there are no guarantees that you will succeed. But if you don't try, how will you know?

Spending the time and doing all the preliminary work that led us to this point is essential, and it will most certainly make a difference compared to if it had not been completed. However, after you have developed a cultural purpose statement, and your culture has been shared and implemented in the organization, the real work begins.

Building a great culture is not dependent on flawlessly executing the ideal strategy and having everything go according to plan. It is all about creating a fully aligned organization and driving widespread behavioral change while overcoming internal barriers, managing energy, and connecting the culture to the business. It also requires that you sustain your culture practice on an ongoing basis and implement not just once-off behaviors but daily, repeated behaviors across the enterprise.

The only way to do this effectively is to place your organization's culture at the center of everything it does. Call it the "Heart of the Business." Be fanatical. Be the coach of your organization, team, and employees, and maintain an open line of communication. Be persistent in demanding the desired behaviors. Make this a daily pursuit that is woven into the fabric of all future endeavors.

As previously mentioned, the next step is to capitalize on the momentum and drive sustainability. The Five-Step Fanatical Framework that follows can help you get started on being fanatical about driving sustainability and embedding your culture as the "Heart of the Business." Make this a part of the DNA of your company. When these five steps are used regularly by everyone in the organization, you are well on your way to building a strong, long-term competitive advantage.

1. Fanatical continuous attention, development, nurturing
2. Fanatical consistency and alignment
3. Fanatical focus on the vital few
4. Fanatical follow-through
5. Fanatical about making the business case

One of the framework's five areas may be more critical to accelerating progress than the others, depending on the current state of your organization. Each of the framework's five components has an important role to play in bringing your culture to life over the long term (Figure 9.1). When combined, the maximum sustained impact is spread throughout the entire organization.

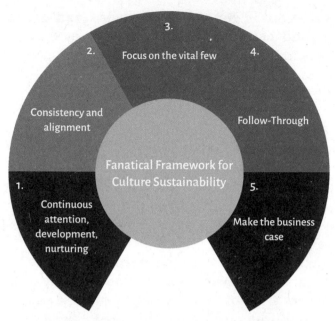

FIGURE 9.1 Fanatical Framework for Culture Sustainability

Five-Step Fanatical Framework

Let's take a closer look at each of the framework's components.

Step #1: Fanatical Continuous Attention, Development, Nurturing

Building culture isn't something you do once a week, once a month, or once a quarter. Your culture needs fanatical continuous attention, development, and nurturing to transform and take shape the way you want it to. It's a continuous pursuit to achieve a winning culture that supports and enhances business performance. There will never be a time when you can look back at the end of the year and say, "O.K., we did enough with our culture. We can stop now." When there is passion and rigor behind continuously building and making your culture better, that sends a powerful message to the rest of the organization.

After the culture has been shared and cascaded throughout the organization, after it has been implemented in all areas, there is a strong tendency for us to assume that the difficult part is over. Many issues that arise during a company's efforts to improve or build a better workplace culture are a result of its segmentation.

One month it may be prioritized, and the next month it may be forgotten about when the pace of business picks up. When there is a lack of focus on continued development, not only do you lose momentum, but your culture is also viewed as a secondary priority. Microsoft CEO Satya Nadella takes the continuous development and building of culture so seriously that he views and operates out of the belief that the "C" in CEO stands for culture. Nadella said, "It's not enough to have a hit product. You must have continuous capability to execute on the next hit product. And that ultimately comes down to culture, having the culture to sustain and foster this capability so you can see around the corners for the next big breakthrough."[2]

Step #2: Fanatical Consistency and Alignment

There must be a consistent message once there is continuous attention, development, and nurturing in your culture, and team members understand that this priority will not change anytime soon. Consistency in not only what is communicated but also the organization's decision-making and daily actions. If your messaging and communication are inconsistent with what the rest of the organization sees daily, you can forget about long-term cultural impact.

I've noticed a few areas of inconsistency that are most common in businesses over the years. If, for example, you communicate that one of your values is trust but your leaders and managers are constantly micromanaging, the behavior statement for this value is unlikely to ever be realized because, clearly, you aren't trusting your employees.

Another example is that you always tell your employees how important culture is, but you rarely or never talk about training and development that are specific to their needs and the culture.

I recently worked with a CEO who was actively trying to improve the culture of his company, and one of the key areas of focus for him was teamwork. It was all about the team. Every message to the organization began and ended with the importance of teamwork. The problem is that this same CEO ignored one individual's poor behavior because of the results that individual was producing. There was no unwavering consistency between what he said and what his actions supported. Leaders and managers must constantly assess the organization's level of consistency. From words and behavior to internal systems and procedures. This is fanatical consistency and alignment!

Step #3: Fanatical Focus on the Vital Few

Attempting to do everything all at once while constantly adding more to the plate is not a great or sustainable action plan. As the months pass, it can be tempting to gather the leadership team or engagement committee and begin laying out a comprehensive portfolio of initiatives in the hopes of achieving cultural excellence. The intention is good but trying to see how many initiatives or projects you can start to keep your culture growing is a losing strategy. The main goal is to identify the vital few areas for improvement that will strengthen your culture while also improving organizational performance.

There is a common trait among leaders and members of culture committees that I've observed over the years that includes a hasty willingness to toss hundreds of ideas, initiatives, and projects into the fire in the hopes that a few will ignite and create a significant impact on the culture. I'll add that this can be enticing. Especially following the launch and implementation of the culture, as discussed in Chapter 8. However, resist the temptation. You'll be glad you did.

It is better and more efficient to focus on a few key areas of growth and impact and then implement and drive the execution of those key areas.

Ask yourself: *What are the vital few areas of improvement in your organization that will have the greatest impact? What are the vital few cultural imperatives that will propel your vision forward?*

Step #4: Fanatical Follow-Through

You must shift your focus to a relentless follow-through once you've decided where you can have the most impact and have identified the vital few cultural imperatives. Starting a tactic or tweaking an existing process or structure is a good place to start, but it is ultimately meaningless unless it is followed through on relentlessly. Not only must you follow-through on what you start and build with zeal, but you must also maintain a firm commitment to keeping culture at the "heart of the business."

Unfortunately, if there isn't a strong emphasis on firm, fanatical, and relentless follow-through, the likelihood of the "start-and-stop" cycle taking over increases dramatically. At some point in your life, you've probably come across the perilous start-stop cycle. It usually consists of starting something while everyone is excited, then abruptly stopping and starting something else due to a distraction. This cycle continues and, in some ways, becomes deeply ingrained in an organization's culture. You can avoid this by making sure that the culture of your company is constantly being developed, improving, and driving to completion what is started.

Without a tenacious and fanatical commitment to bringing your culture to life every day and honoring your original commitments, the risk of culture becoming a "start-and-stop" fad as opposed to a way of being increases significantly.

Step #5: Fanatical About Making the Business Case

Leaders must present a convincing argument for how developing a sustainable culture will enhance business performance and how it is necessary for a long-term impact. This is one of the main reasons why many leaders not only do *not* prioritize culture but also believe that culture has no impact on business performance. When they previously tried to do so, there was most likely a lack of focus on connecting it and deeply embedding it into the business. They become jaded as a result of the lack of impact on the business and move on to something else or delegate it to someone else. The decision to build and improve culture, as well as the time, energy, and resources expended in doing so, is not at fault. The real issue is a failure to integrate culture into the actual business.

To exhibit how your culture can improve business performance, you need to do a lot more than just link your culture to the business. It also requires that leaders deliver compelling and consistent messages about how the culture will benefit not only the company's performance but also the performance of each individual employee. Even if leaders and managers are fully committed to developing and improving their organization's culture, if the correlation between how it will benefit the business and the customers you serve is not made, the sustainability and long-term impact of cultural success will be jeopardized.

Full System Embedment for Sustained Impact

To champion a fanatical, audacious vision from beginning to completion on any path toward transformation or change for the better, a high level of intensity and deep care is required. If you have been implementing the steps presented in this book, then a significant amount of energy, resources, and time has been devoted to reaching this point in your cultural journey. It would be a shame to get this far in your journey only to falter now because you haven't put forward your absolute best when it is needed the most. Unfortunately, I've seen this happen many times in real life, especially when an organization does a great job of launching its culture and giving it inspiration and positive energy, but then falters and loses steam.

During this phase of the process, it is essential to be passionate and fanatical about fostering sustainability and long-term impact through your culture. The most effective way to achieve this is to activate system-wide embedding of not only your culture, but also the best practices and critical few imperatives that will improve cultural performance. Let's assume that by now you have chosen your destination, defined your culture, translated your values into concrete behaviors, and communicated your culture to the rest of the organization.

Don't stop here. It's now time to start instilling your culture in everything you do. The precedent has been established, and hopefully, the anticipation of what could be in the future is growing at this point. It's time to up the ante and ensure that your culture becomes ingrained in the DNA, the "heart" of your organization.

There are several steps in the full system embedment process. Each phase should be meticulously planned and diagnosed before taking any action. The main goal is to build on some of the key areas of focus that you identified when you first launched and implemented your culture.

The following are some strategies for fostering long-term cultural growth and strengthening your organization's culture at a deeper, more fundamental level.

Strategy #1: Rigorous Training and Reinforcement

You get what you train for and regularly reinforce. When it comes to creating a sustainable culture that will have a long-term impact, every little detail counts. Everything an organization does must be done with great intention. However, there is one crucial component that is an absolute necessity. Rigorous training in the context of your culture. The training sessions should be based on the specific behaviors that go along with your values. This will help bring your values to life and put the focus on positive reinforcement of what is expected.

Rather than seeing this as a series of routine or one-time training sessions, it's more about coaching every leader and manager to incorporate the behavioral manifesto into every interaction with direct reports. To begin with, the behavioral statements of your values should be integrated into every existing internal meeting.

Whether it's devoting the first five or ten minutes of the meeting to a discussion of one of your values and the associated behavior statement or focusing the entire meeting on one of the behaviors. From there, each leader and manager should be having regular and frequent coaching conversations with their people on how well they are living the behaviors and bringing them to life. When it comes to specific training, one of the most important factors is for every division in the company to connect the behavioral statements to their daily work and training initiatives.

Championship-winning sports teams, hall-of-famers, and world-class enterprises that consistently win and raise the bar do not achieve greatness solely through talent or strategy. Not only do they train, but the best train and practice more rigorously behind closed doors than they do when the world watches them perform on the big stage. When executive teams and people managers strive for cultural excellence, the same philosophy needs to be applied. There must be consistent, rigorous training to create and sustain the vision and culture that you want throughout the organization. As John C. Maxwell, bestselling author of *Developing the Leader Within You*, stated, "Teamwork makes the dream work, but vision becomes a nightmare when the leader has a big dream and a bad team."[3]

As a leader, you can be passionate about creating the best possible culture and have an extraordinary vision for the workplace you want to create, but without proper training, your dream can quickly become a nightmare. There must be consistent training throughout the organization to achieve the desired behavioral changes.

I am continually amazed by the lack of rigorous training in the business world, especially in areas that are critical to overall business performance and success. When I was given the chance to pursue a lifelong goal of becoming a professional athlete, I was taken aback by the meticulousness with which I had to prepare. A pre-season injury cut short my time playing in the NFL with the Chicago Bears, but it was eye-opening to see the intensity of training in person. As an athlete, I've always taken pride in my dedication and drive to succeed. On the other hand, every player in the NFL was not only talented but also worked just as hard as I did.

As a former linebacker, I had the highest regard for Brian Urlacher and Lance Briggs. I followed their every move. Urlacher was a first-ballot Hall of Famer, and Lance Briggs, I believe, will join him in a few years. But what struck me the most about these two was that they were among the team's hardest workers.

At this point in his career, Brian Urlacher did not need to study and analyze film as much, nor did he need to perfect his craft to the tiniest of details. He amassed a fortune playing a game he cherished and was showered with praise. However, he worked every day to continue enhancing and optimizing his performance. He was fanatical in his pursuit of victory.

In the NFL, everything is not only videotaped, but every detail is scrutinized later that day. Whether you're a ten-year veteran or an undrafted rookie, one obsession is constantly reinforced: to get a little bit better every day.

Every practice is carefully scripted, and every action you take is documented. This may appear excessive or intense in the context of business. I'm not implying that every company trains and develops its employees in the same way that an NFL team does, but there does need to be rigor around training programs and coaching sessions tailored to your company's culture.

In his book, *Excellence Now: Extreme Humanism*, Tom Peters writes, "Training is a capital investment, not a business expense. Ask an admiral, general, fire chief, police chief, football coach, archery coach, theater director, nuclear power plant operations boss, or head of an ER or ICU if you think that's extreme."[4]

Strategy #2: Cultural Impact Committee

A lack of clarity about who will take ownership of the culture and its overall impact on the organization can lead to the beginning of decline. My experience over the years has shown that in order to have a long-term impact on the culture of an organization, it is best to have employees from all divisions and levels working simultaneously with the leadership team and people managers.

Some seem to think that the leadership team should step back and allow HR and an employee resource group (ERG) to take over at this point in the process. A major drawback to this approach is that you risk undermining key organizational imperatives and programs that are already in place. It sends a mixed message to employees when senior leaders and all people managers are heavily involved in culture work at the beginning and then suddenly disappear.

Jamie, a tall woman with a no-nonsense attitude, works in the accounting department of a financial institution that I've been working with for just over a year. Prior to our partnership, the company not only tried to change their culture, but they also went through two other significant company-wide transformations over the years. During a recent lunch break at the company's headquarters, Jamie approached me, held out her hand, and introduced herself. Having a wide range of viewpoints from different parts of an organization I am working with is invaluable. I often hear one thing from the senior leadership team, and then, after some digging and discussions with frontline employees, I am given a completely different perspective and tone. During our brief conversation, I asked, "Jamie, how do you feel about some of the changes taking place at the company?"

"As much as I dislike change at first, these changes that we are making are necessary," she explained. "The issue is that I've been here for eleven years, and we rarely stay committed to long-term change. At first, all leaders are very visible, but their level of visibility disappears over time. Over the years, we've run into issues with delegating major decisions to volunteer employee resource groups. I don't want to be negative, because some of the groups are doing great work, but it hasn't worked for us. It is not uncommon for the group members to be too preoccupied with their work to attend meetings, while others have no idea what they're doing, or simply do not care."

I explained to Jamie that this approach, or one similar to it, not only leads to inefficiency for long-term growth when it comes to major change initiatives but also defeats the purpose of an organization driving sustainable impact. This is not to say that all employee resource groups are bad or do poor work. I've seen many examples of outstanding work by employee resource groups. But are the company's KPIs and strategic direction for a given year delegated to a group of twelve volunteers? Obviously not. Nor should culture.

Knowing that this had previously been the financial institution's downfall, we made a concerted effort to create ownership of the culture while also being very selective in the individuals we chose. The cultural impact committee was formed from this group of team members. Employees from all levels of the organization were represented. Nobody was forced to join the group, and there were no consequences if they didn't.

The top 100 employees in the organization were selected based on their internal ranking system for future potential. The company's CEO would send an invitation to each committee member, explaining the committee's goals and why they were important in the future. These were not only high-performing employees, but most were also very well respected by their coworkers.

It was decided that members of the cultural impact committee would meet with the company's senior leadership team once a month to discuss the company's progress, challenges, and concerns. Having a diverse group of employees on the cultural impact committee helps to uncover issues that senior leaders may not have been aware of until it is too late.

Strategy #3: Define and Prioritize the Cultural Imperatives

Cultural imperatives should be mandated in the same way that organizational imperatives are. Invest in them as much as you would any other important company goal. There are most likely two to five things you can do right now to improve not only the health and performance of your culture but also the overall performance of your company.

Take a moment to reflect on what you've learned. You've hopefully gained some traction and implemented some of the practices from phases two and three of the rollout roadmap in Chapter 8, which helped bring your culture to life when you shared it with the rest of the organization. You may even be able to extend the duration of the practices you assigned in both phases of the roadmap in some cases. If you're satisfied with where your culture is now, it's critical to figure out how to spend your time and energy moving forward.

You've probably heard of the *Pareto Principle*, also known as the 80/20 Principle. The 80/20 rule can also help you take your culture to the next level to sustain and maximize its impact on the rest of your organization. The 80/20 rule simply asserts that 80% of the results or impact of your culture will come from only 20% of the activities or areas of focus. As referenced earlier in the book, acting on a whim and doing one thing after another in the hope that something sticks and makes a difference is not a sustainable strategy. It is not only unsustainable, but it has the potential to backfire in multiple ways and tarnish the progress made thus far.

You might be wondering how you and your team come up with these imperatives and then carry them out. There is no one-size-fits-all approach to determining your cultural imperatives. However, many of the organizations I've worked with over the years have found certain methods to be effective. Let's begin by deciding what those cultural imperatives are. Preliminary research will be necessary, but the payoff will be well worth the time invested. The goal is to figure out which imperatives will have the most effect on your business and help your culture move forward.

Discovering what is causing the most friction in your company and what can be done to alleviate it is a good place to start. Invite employees to participate in a short survey to provide input on the most significant areas of impact. Members of the cultural impact committee and HR executives can conduct quick pulse checks around the company while the survey is being distributed to identify different pressure points. The emphasis is to approach this collaboratively without judgment.

It's critical to understand that when I speak of cultural imperatives, I'm not referring to one-off projects. What I'm referring to are the practices and functions that are integral to both the organization's cultural growth and its commercial success. Some examples include tying the culture to onboarding, talent development, leadership development, knowledge sharing, commercial capability training, and mentoring programs. For each organization, the situation and findings will be unique.

Senior leaders and the cultural impact committee should rank the cultural imperatives based on their importance to the organization and where it is currently situated. They might, for instance, receive eight recommendations for cultural imperatives. They must decide which two or three imperatives will have the greatest impact on organizational performance and the implementation path for each imperative. Assume that in the next six months, there will be three imperatives implemented. Each cultural imperative should have a detailed plan in place for each of the initiatives and practices that will help implement it.

Each member of the cultural impact committee will be assigned to one of several groups after the discovery of the cultural impact areas, with senior leaders and managers following suit. Each group will be in charge of coming up with a plan and putting the chosen cultural imperative into action.

Strategy #4: Handbook of Cultural Guidelines

A team handbook was always one of the first things I received upon reporting to training camp throughout my football career, whether it was in college or the NFL. It's common for the culture's handbook to be an entire section of the playbook or even separate from the playbook itself. Even though the message of "how things are done around here" will be repeated in the coming months, each player is given a physical copy. You'll never be without this guide. Every team meeting, every position meeting, and every day before the start of each meeting, your coaches will refer to a theme in the handbook.

In my travels around the world, I have been surprised by how many organizations do not distribute a handbook of cultural guidelines to all employees. An employee handbook is not what I'm referring to, but rather a detailed cultural handbook that outlines your company's culture and behavioral expectations for each employee. For example, the Behavioral Manifesto and a Q&A section on what to do and whom to contact if something specific occurs could be included.

Reaffirming and clarifying expectations and alignment around the company's culture are two major goals of this cultural handbook. Like everything else in this book, nothing will build your culture on its own. However, having a year-round reference guide to cultural guidelines can be extremely helpful in reinforcing important aspects that contribute to long-term cultural growth. It also sends a strong message to other employees that this is not a half-hearted attempt to improve the company's culture. It's everywhere. It's all connected.

Strategy #5: Ignite and Inspire Your Teams

Research shows just how critical it is to inspire employees and how an inspired workforce can significantly improve an organization's productivity. Leaders from around the world were surveyed and asked to rate the productivity of their employees in four different categories: workers who were dissatisfied with their jobs, satisfied workers, engaged workers, and finally, inspired workers. The findings paint a clear picture of the productive force of inspired employees. Not only are inspired employees more productive, but it would take close to three satisfied employees to produce the same amount of output as one inspired employee. What did researchers find as the best source of inspiration for a workforce? Utilize the company's mission to give work meaning and direction.[5]

How can you begin to inspire your organization around your culture? Start by telling inspiring stories about your company's culture and how its values and core principles have impacted employees, customers, and other key stakeholders. You can take it a step further by finding a creative way to publish or create a keepsake that can be distributed to every employee, including new hires, and that can be updated on a regular basis with new and more inspiring examples.

Discover Financial is a good example of a company that reinforces its values by telling inspiring stories about how living those values at work has impacted employees. They have written a 100-plus-page book that they call their *Culture Book*. Discover's culture book shares not only their values and core principles, but also stories and examples of how employees have lived by those values.[6]

Not only will your culture be strengthened, but your employees will also be more impacted when they hear positive and inspiring stories about how the culture or living the organization's values has positively affected other colleagues. There are various approaches to ignite and inspire around your organization's culture. But there is one thing I am certain of. The more you can tell stories and share positive examples of how your company's values and principles have touched and impacted your people, the more likely it is that your culture will not be short-lived.

Strategy #6: Create an Environment of Recognition

During my meeting with the CEO and the CHRO of an agricultural company, we discussed some internal headwinds that were affecting business performance. The company has been losing key employees who were seen as the company's future for the past few months, and morale was terrible. Much worse than they realized.

The CEO and CHRO were shocked when I told them that one of the alarming observations I made while watching their division heads and managers conduct internal meetings was the lack of enthusiasm and recognition for employees doing great things. I suggested that they start recognizing and praising great work by employees right away to help set the tone for everyone else. The CEO's first response was, "Why would we recognize and praise their efforts for what they are supposed to be doing?"

Many executives and managers share this sentiment. In some ways, I completely understand. I really do. It can feel way too touchy-feely but let me give you an example of how being *fanatical* about creating an environment of employee recognition can change the long-term impact of your culture in a big way.

Yum! Brands, Inc.'s co-founder and former chairman and CEO is David Novak. From 1999 to January 2016, he served as CEO. During Novak's time at Yum! Brands, the company doubled its restaurant count to 41,000, increased its market value from just under $4 billion to almost $32 billion, and became a leader in its sector for return on invested capital. They were regarded as one of the best financial performers in the business world at that time.

Inquiring minds wonder about a man like this. *What made Novak so successful?* The majority of his time and attention was devoted to his employees and recognizing the people responsible for the company's great success. Reporters have noted how Novak's office looked back when he was CEO. His office was littered with rubber chickens, plastic hogs, and other toys. Photos of Novak with friends and customers adorned the walls of his office. He was fixated on the lives of everyday people, his employees, not celebrities or presidents. The company's success had always rested on Novak's team-building philosophy.

This philosophy centered primarily on creating an environment of constant recognition in the workplace. As an example, Novak created the *Rubber Chicken Award* while he was in charge of KFC. Leaders from all over would frequently ask Novak what the secret ingredient to their culture was, to which he would respond, "We took recognition and had more fun with it than most people." Managers at Yum! Brands continue to honor the tradition today. The unique aspect of how they recognize employees, however, is that it is done instantly. There is no need to wait for an official award. During a meeting, if an employee does an outstanding job, the manager will take a break and publicly recognize that employee and hand them their Yum award right there on the spot.[7]

When Novak appeared on CNBC, he said that people crave consistent and constant praise from their managers. Also, he said that while it is important to recognize employees for their achievements, there must also be a deliberate effort to recognize the behavior that is unacceptable.[8]

Strategy #7: Mentoring and Coaching

Mentoring and coaching can have a significant impact on both the culture of a company and its ability to perform. Especially when it comes to creating a long-term organizational culture of sustainability and impact. Using SGWS-IL as an example, highly focused mentoring and coaching were a core tenet of driving long-term change with their "Get Better Today . . . Together" culture and fully embedding it. The goal was not only to introduce high-potential employees to senior management and increase their knowledge, but also to provide a medium for walking through the culture, specifically the behavioral manifesto.

Once a month, each senior leader in the company met with a director or manager from a different division to conduct mentoring sessions. These started out as simple Zoom or phone calls, but as time went on, people began meeting for lunch and others went well beyond the allotted time for their calls, which was encouraging. Six months after being mentored by a senior leader, division directors and managers would then turn around and mentor others. For the next six months, the senior leaders would undertake mentoring sessions with a new group.

The primary and most essential guidelines were:

- To build cross-divisional unity. The leaders did everything they could to ensure that the pairings included people from different divisions.

- To actively engage in career conversations about future goals, career development, and addressing challenges or questions as they arise.
- To discuss the "Get Better Today . . . Together" culture and provide examples of positive daily behaviors outlined in the Behavioral Manifesto.

Addressing those three components was critical in driving full system embedment of the culture. The discussions were both effective and beneficial, but they also continued to send a message that the focus on culture would be fanatical and ongoing.

Strategy #8: Connect Culture to Learning and Development

As we discussed earlier in this chapter, rigorous training is essential for both developing a deeper understanding of the culture and driving business performance. In a similar vein, leaders should make it a top priority to create a world-class learning organization.

Almost every company has a learning and development team with a portal of ongoing learning goals, but the real question is how well learning and development are tied to the company's culture and how well they drive business performance. I see a lot of organizations where their learning and development work is not connected to their culture in any way, and there is no alignment on the evolving capabilities that are needed to drive business performance. This is a common problem.

Using and structuring your learning and development programs can be a great way to build a long-term impact culture. Pfizer is a great example of how a strong and effective learning and development focus can pay enormous dividends.

Pfizer's Head of Learning and Development, Sean Hudson, is leading the company's efforts to build the future of work through a strong emphasis on learning and development. Three types of learning have been identified by Pfizer, which they cultivate and incorporate into all their efforts. These include required learning, necessary learning, and desired learning. Because Pfizer operates in a highly regulated industry, there is a great deal of learning that is *required*. The *necessary learning* focuses on the specific skills and competencies that will help employees succeed in their roles. The *desired learning* consists of providing employees with the opportunity to learn about areas of interest to them.

Sean also stressed the significance of linking Pfizer's four core values to the foundation of their learning and development efforts in an interview with Lydia Abbot at LinkedIn. Sean said, "Skills in and of themselves are great and important to have. But we need those skills to live in the context of our values. We need them to live in the context of the role. We need them to live and have an application to something more than just the acquisition of the skill, or the acquisition of the knowledge."

As a result, Pfizer is constantly looking for ways to free employees and give them the opportunity to keep learning. You can't simply tell employees that learning is important; you also have to make time for them to do so.[9]

Action Steps to Be Fanatical About Sustained Impact with Your Culture

1. **Fierce fanatical approach:** The only way to truly build a culture that is sustainable and has a long-term impact is to be fanatical about culture cultivation. I know I've said it over and over again in this book, but I can't stress it enough: No one thing or one aspect is enough to build a culture. Leaders who are fierce and fanatical in their culture-building efforts will inspire others to do the same.

2. **Fanatical mindset of the long game:** Building a company's culture is a long-term endeavor. It's critical that you constantly remind yourself that short-term gain must never come at the expense of your culture's long-term health and growth.

3. **Fanatical process-driven:** While planning and strategizing for both short-term and long-term cultural impact are critical, it is also vital to reverse engineer your attention to the daily process. To build championship-caliber, growing, and productive teams, you must fanatically commit to the process and do the necessary little things consistently over time.

4. **Use the Five-Step Fanatical Framework:** Use the *Five-Step Fanatical Framework* for long-term cultural impact as a starting point to plan how you and your organization will implement it. Think about it. How can each step of the framework be aligned with a clear direction and strategy for the upcoming six to twelve months?

5. **Fanatical full system embedment:** Implement the eight shared strategies for full system embedment listed in this chapter. Determine which strategies and focus areas will have the greatest impact. At the end of the day, it all boils down to you and your company. Even though the strategies listed above are extremely effective when implemented, they are not the be-all and end-all. The most important thing is to maintain a consistent focus on generating and maintaining long-term cultural impact.

CHAPTER 10

The Ultimate Differentiator Is Leadership

There are only two ways to influence human behavior.
You can manipulate it, or you can inspire it.

—Simon Sinek, author of *Start with Why*

The ultimate differentiator in any organization is the performance and effectiveness of its leaders. If two equally talented teams or businesses compete in the same market, the team or business with the more effective leaders will prevail. And when it comes to changing the culture of an organization or making it a more inspiring and high-performing place to work, the ultimate impact and success will depend on how well the organization's leaders collectively work together.

This cannot be avoided. This cannot be denied. This cannot be overlooked. Nothing can make up for a lack of leadership performance. How a company's leaders act daily, how they interact with and treat others, and the examples they set send a strong message to the rest of the organization to follow suit.

When assessing an IPO, 90% of investors believe that the performance and quality of an organization's leadership team form the most important factor. When the leadership team works together toward a common vision, the probability of exceeding the median financial performance increases by 1.9 times.[1]

Most people are aware that leaders are important during change efforts, especially when there is a change in culture. However, many still underestimate the overall influence and impact that all leaders have. But I've learned over many years that it's often the leaders themselves who don't fully realize how much influence they have on change initiatives.

This can be said for almost everything, though, not just change initiatives or enhancing the cultural performance of an organization. When the leader improves, everything benefits.

Dan Cathy, the former CEO of Chick-fil-A and current Chairman of the Board, recalls sending out a customer survey in Dallas early in his career. In the survey, 25% of customers said they would not return to Chick-fil-A. When looking at the responses of customers who said they wouldn't return, there were a variety of reasons given. Cathy's first reaction was to complain and press the business operators and owners even harder. As time passed, he realized that his strategy was yielding little results.

One day, when a book appeared on his desk, it marked a turning point in his professional life. *Quality Is Free* was the title of the book by Phillip Crosby. Cathy remembered a phrase in the book that would change everything for him. "What is in the business is a reflection of leadership." Dan Cathy realized that yelling at business operators and telling owners to do a better job had little relevance in comparison to himself growing and improving as a leader. Cathy became an avid learner after that. The more he learned and grew as a leader, the better the company became.[2]

When I first start working with an organization, whether to help them transform their culture or provide leadership development training, I can get a good sense of the organization's future potential by just watching and interacting with the leaders. If an organization's collective leadership is weak or unhealthy in any way, that organization's vision is not likely to be realized unless there is a change in leadership or a strong focus on leadership development and growth.

On the other hand, an organization's chances of success are exponentially higher than those of other teams if it has noble goals and aspirations and its leadership team is made up of high-performing leaders who trust one another. Even if an organization has an excellent product or world-class service, its long-term success and impact will be limited if its leadership team is insufficient. It is possible for an organization to have or do nearly everything else immaculately but still fall short due to poor leadership.

Consider the case of a struggling organization that undergoes a merger and new ownership takes over. What is one of the first things that happens almost immediately? Most of the time, the current leadership team is disbanded, and new leadership is appointed to serve the organization's future. This is because, regardless of the complexity of a situation or the contributing factors that led to the company's decline, the performance of the leaders got them there in the first place. It's a harsh reality, and in some cases, some of those leaders may even be terrific individuals who are well liked throughout the organization. But just because someone may be well respected doesn't mean they should stick around, especially if the organization's performance has been severely struggling.

"Everything rises and falls on leadership," says bestselling author John Maxwell, and I couldn't agree more. The overall performance of an organization, its cultural excellence or lack thereof, are directly related to the competency and performance of its leaders. I am so convinced of this that it is one of the main reasons I spend most of my time with the leadership team when I first start working with a company. Even if the end goal isn't always aimed solely at the executive team, it always starts and ends there for a reason. That's because the top executives' forces at work can make or break a company.

I've seen plenty of examples over the years where a company was in prime position to execute their cultural change as planned, but everything ended up collapsing due to the ego and lack of commitment of a few leaders. One leader can't build a team or change an entire organization, but one leader can certainly break a team and destroy the culture. Therefore, it is imperative that all leaders in a company preparing to improve or change its culture are aligned and willing to enhance their own leadership effectiveness.

As a preface to the discussion of the leader's role in building culture and how to lead the transformation of changing culture, I'd like to share some thoughts on leadership in general:

- Leadership is more than just a title. The ability and desire to have a positive impact on the lives of others are what leadership is all about. It's not about a title or a position; it's about your ability to positively influence the lives of others. There are some individuals who hold the title of boss, but they are far from being true leaders. Others may not have the official title, but they demonstrate an extraordinary ability to make a difference in the lives of others, and when they speak, people listen. Leading does not imply directing and telling others where to go or what to do, but rather blazing a trail and progressing first.

- Leadership is not only essential but indispensable. Leadership is an enormous responsibility that must never be taken lightly. Not only are all eyes on you and your every move scrutinized, but the families and livelihoods of those you lead are dependent on your ability to show up every day and excel in your actions. A simple thank-you note, or positive recognition or acknowledgment, can change the entire course of someone's day, and possibly even their life.

- No number of good intentions, plans, or strategies will ever be able to compensate for, or replace, poor leadership. Every company should devote as much time and thought to developing leaders as it does to strategy and finances. While the senior leadership team's performance is vital, the goal should be to create a leadership factory: a workplace where even new employees and those without a title know they can lead and make a difference right where they are.

A Leader's Role in Building Culture

During the process of building culture and taking organizational performance to the next level, leaders must excel in a variety of aspects and key responsibilities. There is not one area that is more valuable than another. An often-asked question over the years has been, "What are the most important things for leaders to do when it comes to building culture, and which part of the process is most important?" That is a slightly complicated question because everything a leader does during the journey of creating a better culture, at every stage of the process, is vital.

At the start of the journey, the leaders of an organization are the ones who instill the culture's direction and communicate the vision. It is then up to the leaders at the halfway point of the journey to role model the desired behaviors to embed the culture in a more profound and meaningful way. It does not end there. Once the culture has been introduced to the organization and all its employees, it is up to the leaders not only to continue to live the values but also to connect the culture in an inspiring way that makes it the heart and soul of the company.

Is it solely dependent on the leaders whether an organization's culture is transformed or significantly improved? Of course not. On the other hand, though, undervaluing how much is decided based on the performance of the organization's leaders amid change initiatives has prevented many companies from achieving their desired results.

The whole discussion about how important leaders are to an organization's success and their ability to build a world-class culture can sometimes send the wrong message. I was recently in Palm Beach, Florida, working with a client to advise them in the final stages of their complete cultural transformation. Things had been going according to plan up until this point. They had experienced some rough patches along the way, but they were moving in the right direction.

The company had developed a cultural purpose statement that piqued everyone's interest from the start and provided a much-needed spark of enthusiasm as the journey progressed. The leaders undertook the difficult but necessary task of completely reshaping their core values and turning them into specific behavioral statements. They embraced a leadership team and a group of people managers who were enthusiastic about the company's future and did everything according to specific guidelines. When it came time to introduce the culture to the company and launch the new identity of how things would be executed from now on, their efforts were lauded by all employees, for the most part. From there, they integrated their new culture into the operations of the business and identified the vital few cultural imperatives that would drive extraordinary impact.

Based on this, you may be asking why I'm sharing this with you because it seems like everything was moving along smoothly. "So, what's the problem?" you're saying to yourself.

"Today was great, but I have just one question," a leader named Monica said at the end of a leadership meeting we had that afternoon in Florida at a local hotel. "Isn't it time for the leadership team to take a step back and allow others to take the lead? We have disrupted our normal working practices for nine months to successfully drive the culture change, but I believe it is time to pass the torch."

Monica's question that afternoon reflected what others were thinking. Three other leaders stood up and agreed with Monica's remarks after she finished speaking. Even though only four of the fifty leaders in the room spoke up, I could tell that every executive in the room that afternoon was eagerly awaiting my response.

"You are absolutely correct," I replied. "Every leader in this room has done an exceptional job, but the responsibility of fully owning and shaping your culture has no expiration date. Everyone here today has changed their working methods and leadership styles in some way, and I applaud you all for it. Inspiring and coaching others to join you in paving the way forward are extremely crucial, but your role as a culture driver does not end here."

I wanted to share that example because it's critical to understand that when focusing on the role of the leader during culture change, it must be an ongoing pursuit for the rest of their career, not just for a few months or years. When heavy emphasis is placed on leaders, others may misinterpret the meaning. They may believe that the leaders are being elevated to a higher status and importance and that everyone else is insignificant.

However, this is the furthest thing from the truth. Everyone matters and is valuable, especially when it comes to the difficult task of building and creating a more high-performing culture. It's just that, as a leader, the ability to create and influence meaningful change in a company is second to none. The goal is for all employees, managers, and non-managers alike to lead by example and demonstrate daily the very fabric that makes up your culture.

But the vision must come first before all of this, which is described further in this chapter. Employees will always look to the leaders of an organization first to envision the way forward, lead the way forward, and maintain a strong belief in the possibilities of the way forward. That is why a strong emphasis on leaders must be placed at every stage of the process and continue to be displayed every step of the way forward.

Employees will begin to look elsewhere for cues on how to behave if an organization's leaders do not make a strong

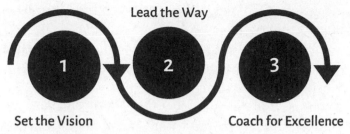

Lead the Way

Set the Vision

Coach for Excellence

FIGURE 10.1   A Leader's Role in Building Culture

commitment to doing what they ask of others on a regular basis. And when that happens, the results are usually the exact opposite of what every leader wants.

Having said that, let's delve deeper into the specific actions and responsibilities for leaders in the pursuit of building or changing culture. It doesn't matter if you're a senior executive, a people manager, or a frontline supervisor (see Figure 10.1).

There will be plenty of other responsibilities along the way, some of which will be unexpected, but there are three actions that are critical in driving cultural impact and change.

Action #1: Set the Vision

The one job of leaders that no one else can do is to set the vision of the culture and to relentlessly share the specifics of that vision, communicate it, and illustrate clear examples of how to enact it every single day. Leaders who understand the importance of vision and then over-communicate that vision are the best builders of culture. Speaking of vision may come off as trite and even corny to some, but the most effective business leaders and sports coaches talk about these all the time and for a good reason. *Because it matters*. It only appears soft and cringeworthy when there is no substance behind the words.

Not only that, but companies that struggle and never seem to gain traction don't devote the time and effort necessary to develop a vision that everyone can understand and initiate. Quantitative and difficult-to-understand metrics will not move the needle. People connect with stories, and the most successful businesses can often tell their cultural change story in a few paragraphs or less.[3]

Setting a successful vision requires not only communicating the vision for your culture early on, but also continuously painting a clear image of where the company is, where it is going, and how the company is going to get there. When leaders can passionately communicate the cultural vision and tie it back to how each team member plays a specific role in contributing to it, the vision begins to stick and gain traction.

Action #2: Lead the Way Forward

When you have established a cultural North Star—a vision of where you want to go and the organizational environment you want to create—you must take charge and lead the way forward. All successful turnarounds, company-wide transformations, or culture changes are only possible because leaders press ahead and blaze the trail. To break through resistance and truly change the direction of an organization, leaders must make a firm commitment to charge forward first. It's a recipe for disaster and mediocrity to communicate your vision and the type of culture you want to create while expecting others to change their ways of working if you remain stagnant. It's a recipe for disaster to expect others to change their behavior to help create the culture that leaders are promoting while they remain the same.

Sadly, this is a common strategy for leaders. Then, after a failed attempt at leading a change initiative or transforming the culture, there are roundtable discussions as a leadership team to try to figure out where things went wrong. The worst part is that fingers, rather than thumbs, are usually pointed. Before an organization can get its employees to buy into its culture or engage in the specific behaviors that help bring the values to life, it must conduct an honest and serious assessment of how well each leader is modeling the behaviors themselves and how effective they are at following their cultural North Star. The behavior of the organization mirrors your behavior as a leader.

Action #3: Coach for Excellence

Every change leader's playbook should include ongoing and frequent coaching when driving culture change. It is not enough to communicate what you want others to begin doing or what needs to occur in the organization. The best leaders who get the most out of their teams identify as coaches rather than managers or leaders. Coaching as a leader is so important that some organizations, such as the WD-40 Company, go so far as to call every manager in the company a coach rather than a manager.[4] The point isn't whether you *call* every manager a coach. What matters is that every leader has a thorough understanding of the culture and what it stands for, models the behavioral shifts, and focuses heavily on coaching others to do the same. Coaching is a critical part of effective leadership.

When I reflect on my entire athletic career, there was one common trait in every coach that had a significant impact on my life, not only as an athlete but also as a man. They were there with me in the trenches, helping me to discover my own potential and what I was capable of, even when I didn't realize it myself.

That kind of self-discovery is only possible when someone is not only in your corner but also by your side every step of the way. Sure, they had the title of coach, but there are plenty of coaches in sports who don't coach and instead shout and just manage. Becoming an authentic and effective coach is a conscious decision that is made every day.

Become a Transformational Leader Now

In today's fast-paced business environment, creating a winning culture demands more than a little tweaking. What is needed is a full transformation of existing processes and systems that will no longer aid the organization in winning and enhancing its performance. It's imperative to change old and outdated mind-sets that no longer serve the path forward.

Constantly analyze and search for ways to transform in order to move faster, become more agile, and develop a sense of urgency. Most importantly, what's needed more than anything else is transformational leadership. Transformational leadership is one of the most studied leadership styles. It has been studied and talked about for decades.

James V. Downtown, a sociologist, coined the term *transformational leadership* in the early 1970s. From there, many people have contributed to the concept, which has grown in popularity over time. James Burns, a biographer of US presidents, expanded on the concept in 1978. The work of leadership expert Bernard Bass, who was inspired by Burns's work, helped to popularize transformational leadership even further.[5]

Bernard Bass and Roland Riggio defined transformational leadership in their 2006 book, *Transformational Leadership*, as

> *Those who stimulate and inspire followers to both achieve extraordinary outcomes and, in the process, develop their own leadership capacity. Transformational leaders help followers grow and develop into leaders by responding to individual followers' needs by empowering them and by aligning the objectives and goals of the individual followers, the leader, the group, and the larger organization.*[6]

Transformational leadership has the potential not only to produce exceptional business and organizational results but also to completely transform the lives of employees. It is extremely difficult to completely change culture, improve culture, or even maintain an already strong culture. A little tweaking here and there, along with some minor changes in approach, will not produce the results that are desired. Leaders need to display the best version of themselves and be ready to transform the lives of the people they lead if they want to transform the organization.

Is it true that some leaders are more gifted than others in terms of inspiring their teams and the entire workforce? Without a doubt, outliers and once-in-a-generation talents will always exist in life, just as they do in everything else. Some of the greatest athletes in history were so gifted at such a young age that everyone around them just knew they were going to be stars one day. The same can be said of legendary musicians or even famous movie stars.

Those who have been singing or acting since the age of 4. They often make it appear so simple to others. Those athletes, musicians, actors, and even some of history's greatest leaders are, however, not the norm. Just because those individuals exist doesn't mean that someone can't grow and develop to a world-class level if they don't have the same skill set at an early age. The same is true of leadership. No matter where you are in your leadership journey, I believe you have an infinite amount of potential waiting to be unlocked and unleashed into the world.

Not long ago, I was speaking with an HR leader about specific leaders within the organization who were not performing to the best of their abilities. "We have to be honest here," this HR leader said to me after thirty minutes of our conversation. "Some people are born with the leadership gene, while others are not. I don't believe that great leadership can be taught."

I respectfully disagree with that statement wholeheartedly. I have seen first-hand the transformation that can occur when a leader's heart is in the right place, receives the right guidance, and becomes inspired. One of the greatest privileges of my work over the last decade has been traveling the world and interacting with some of the world's most extraordinary leaders. It comes up almost every time that who they were as a leader ten or even twenty years ago isn't even close to who they are now.

Horst Schulze, cofounder of the Ritz-Carlton Hotel Company, admitted that, early in his career, he showed little promise as a leader. He claims that anyone can develop the inner strength to become a great leader over time if they can first lead themselves well.[7]

There will always be naturally gifted leaders and managers with a rare gift for developing others, outstanding people skills, or exceptional emotional intelligence. That should never deter another leader who does not currently have the same skill set from taking the leap and striving to become a transformational leader.

Transformational leadership sounds great in theory, but how does it work in practice? How can a leader or people manager actively engage in a set of actions or processes that will not only increase their influence but also help them become transformational? There are four components to bringing transformational leadership to life and making the most of your impact as a leader for cultural change (see Figure 10.2).

A leader must first undergo transformation before he or she can transform others or the organization. The transformation of a leader enables them to then transform others. When an organization's people are transformed, the culture is also transformed. When the culture is transformed, the organization itself becomes transformed. When organizational transformation takes root, performance vastly improves, increasing profits and satisfying key stakeholders.

Let's take a look at each of the four areas and see what specific steps can be taken to help jumpstart each process.

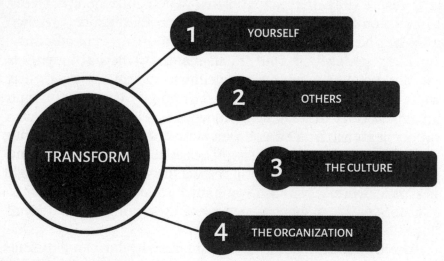

FIGURE 10.2 Transformational Leadership Framework

Part #1: Transforming Yourself

It all begins with the transformation of the leader. When a leader undergoes transformation, extraordinary things begin to unfold. When that number is multiplied, and one transformed leader becomes ten or twenty transformed leaders, the organizational impact is even greater. The goal for any organization should be to keep increasing the number of transformed leaders.

When you see a leader who has a special way about them, from how they communicate, inspire others, and drive the business, often an internal transformation of some sort has occurred before there were visible external results. The goal is to keep raising that number, depending on the size of the organization. This is because, at its core, leadership is a transfer of impact. The more a leader is influenced and changed in their own life, the greater their impact and influence on others.

Self-transformation can take place in a variety of ways. Some leaders become transformed, and their lives are forever changed when they experience a personal tragedy that brings them to their knees. Others may be energized and become a man or woman on a mission after failing and facing adversity. Others may have a health scare that makes them realize how short life is, while another leader may become a lifelong learner who loves growing and getting better all the time.

When properly channeled, all these examples can serve as building blocks for self-transformation. The bottom line is that there are countless ways for leaders to become transformed, and what works for one leader may not work for another. However, for one to be transformed, there does not need to be a life-changing event or a catastrophic failure. It's easy to think of transformation as an all-out effort, but it all begins with making the right next move with intentionality. Transformation is an evolutionary process. The path starts with a relentless pursuit to grow and become a better version of yourself, consistently pressing outside of your comfort zone and learning more about your own unique strengths.

Carol Dweck, a world-renowned Stanford psychologist and best-selling author of the book *Mindset*, has dedicated her life to studying what distinguishes the highly successful from everyone else. Even though talent, background, resources, and a variety of other factors all play a role, it is one's mindset that makes the most difference. According to Dweck's research, it all comes down to whether one has a growth or fixed mindset. When someone has a fixed mindset, they believe their talent and current skill set are predetermined and beyond their control. A growth mindset, on the other hand, is the polar opposite. One can grow and develop over time, regardless of circumstances, background, or current skill level. Another important aspect of a growth or fixed mindset is how one responds to adversity. A fixed mindset will frequently seek to assign blame rather than use their challenge or adversity to grow. Someone with a growth mindset believes that they can improve and grow from the difficult experience they are currently going through.[8]

Carol Dweck's work, and the adoption of a growth mindset, have gained traction in companies all over the world, including many major corporations, over the years. Some companies have even incorporated it into their mission statements. Employees at companies that have implemented a growth mindset report feeling more inspired and dedicated to the overall mission. Employees at a fixed-mindset company, on the other hand, report more inappropriate and toxic behavior. In organizations that have not only adopted a growth mindset but also practice it daily, appropriate risk-taking is encouraged and even praised. Developing and implementing a growth mindset are not an easy task, but the benefits for leaders and organizations can be enormous.[9]

As a leader, developing a deeper understanding of the growth mindset can provide you with the necessary tools to begin the process of self-transformation. How does this apply to leading a culture change or enhancing your organization's culture? Given that changing or improving an organization's culture entails large-scale behavioral change, regularly evaluating yourself and direct reports to see if you are living the values is a good place to start.

Transforming yourself as a leader is also driven by a strong desire to learn and grow outside of the office. Do you have a personal development plan outlining how and when you intend to grow? Transforming yourself demands that you constantly strive to be a little better than the day before, rather than relying on past success or accomplishments. Those moments of incremental progress begin to add up over time. And the accumulation of those growth moments begins to transform you as a person, how you lead, and the impact of your leadership over time.

Part #2: Transforming Others

When a leader makes a firm commitment to grow and develop on a continuous basis, not only does their leadership effectiveness improve, but so does their ability to influence and transform others. The most effective leaders do not view transforming others as a separate objective from their daily responsibilities. Since they have done the work on themselves and are advocates for practicing what they preach, teaching and coaching others to do the same become second nature.

A critical component of transforming others is understanding that everyone you lead or work with has a unique set of strengths and is challenged in different ways. This is important to remember because, far too often, leaders and people managers will take a one-size-fits-all approach, which is no longer acceptable. Advancing into the future and leading effectively through change require an acute understanding of your team members' most pressing needs and then advising on the best way to meet those needs.

When it comes to successfully leading cultural change, a leader must first understand where his or her team members are and what adjustments must be made to align with the culture. It is not necessary to tell people what to do differently once they understand where they are now and where they need to go. Meeting with those team members one-on-one and asking the right questions are even more necessary.

When we consider inspiring or transforming another individual, we are naturally drawn to believe that it consists of what we must do. Often, however, it is more about asking the right questions and actively listening. The more we listen and are able to identify pain points through facial expressions or body language, the better prepared we are to drive maximum impact. As a leader, you are not a therapist or psychologist, so no one expects you to know what's going on in each team member's mind. But it's amazing what can be revealed over time when a leader is consistent and intentional about driving a deeper connection with those they lead and getting to know them better.

The true value of getting to know team members on a deeper level in relation to transformation is that if you don't understand what's important to them, inspiring and moving them become extremely difficult. Even if a significant number of employees are inspired and enthusiastic about the culture and messaging that has been communicated, this will not be the case for everyone. Leaders will never be able to convert everyone in the organization, but it's critical for those who are halfway in and halfway out to connect the organizational purpose to their own. To do this, you must know not only what the team members' professional goals and aspirations are, but also what their personal goals and aspirations are.

Matthew Kelly, a friend, and *New York Times* bestselling author, wrote *The Dream Manager*, a game-changing book.[10] The book is based on the idea that when an organization and its leaders assist employees in achieving personal goals, the organization benefits directly. When leaders care about their team members' professional aspirations as well as their personal development, it empowers employees to want to bring their best for their employer.

Part #3: Transforming the Culture

When an organization's leaders are committed to growing and transforming themselves, as well as regularly transforming others, it has a direct impact on and begins to transform the company's culture. A transformed culture is the result of transformed people who routinely transform others. As previously stated, leaders will never be able to obtain complete and total buy-in when attempting to build a stronger and better culture.

Too many leaders spend way too much time and energy on the employees who cause them the most problems. Employees who, no matter how hard a leader tries to guide them, will most likely be those who will never change. That is not only a waste of time, but it also interferes with what is most important: spending time on those who want to change but haven't decided on their direction yet.

Given that culture is defined by what an organization repeatedly does daily, cultural transformation occurs when one more individual transforms his or her behavior to align with the culture. Each person who changes their behavior adds to the total number of people who have altered their behavior in a month. The more that number rises each month, the more cultural growth and change become apparent.

Sometimes, when an organization lays out a bold plan to change or transform their culture, it can overwhelm leaders, given their current workload. A simpler and more effective way to think about it is to consider assisting one member of your team who hasn't quite made the shift yet in making the desired change. Not only does this alleviate pressure, but it also connects leaders to the daily process of taking one small step in the right direction. Not only can this mindset pay huge dividends, but when all leaders and people managers adopt a similar mindset, the results can be transformative. To maximize its effectiveness, who are the influencers and superstar employees who have already fully embraced the culture? Figure out who those individuals are and encourage them to follow suit.

As a leader or manager, you must constantly remind yourself of what you have control over and where you can have the most impact. Thinking about changing everything and everyone from the beginning will not only derail morale but will also interfere with the difference you can make right now. A transformational leader's mindset is always asking how they can go out and impact one person through the culture for that day.

Part #4: Transforming the Organization

Organizational performance is transformed when leaders transform themselves and others, which directly influences cultural transformation. All four parts of the framework for bringing transformational leadership to life are critical to driving cultural success. The four parts are intertwined and linked. They all feed off one another, and when one is missing or deficient, it makes it more difficult to excel in another.

Transformational leaders elevate a shared purpose toward driving total organizational growth, even if they oversee a specific division or function of the business. Everyone benefits in some way when the company becomes more successful and grows. Transformational leaders want their direct teams to succeed and set an example for all other teams, but the company's success is the most important thing to them. This necessitates a consistent focus on eliminating bureaucratic tendencies and silos that prevent cross-functional collaboration. When leaders concentrate on improving and excelling in these four areas, the path to becoming a transformational leader becomes not only more attainable but also more impactful.

Build a Leadership Factory

With the importance of leadership in creating an exceptional culture, I am always surprised by how little time and resources an organization devotes to developing and growing its leaders. Every facet of an organization benefits from a strong emphasis on the development and growth of its leaders. It's not just the culture.

I was on a discovery call with an organization last month that hired me to not only keynote an upcoming executive conference but also provide six months of leadership training afterward. I hadn't started working with the company yet, but as part of my due diligence prior to our first event together, I tried to dig as deep as possible to gain a thorough understanding of the target audience. Gareth, the CEO, and his chief of staff were on the discovery call. When I asked Gareth what their biggest challenge was, he replied that other leaders and managers needed to improve their feedback skills.

I didn't interrupt him; I was all ears, listening to him rant for fifteen minutes about his dissatisfaction with their ability to provide effective feedback. After he finished speaking, I inquired as to whether they currently offered any sort of ongoing and frequent leadership or managerial development program.

"We have considered it," Gareth responded, "but we simply haven't had the time."

What? I thought to myself. *That's a bunch of crap*. I mean this with all due respect, and I made similar remarks to Gareth that day after he confided this.

If you lack time to develop leaders but have time to complain about them being inefficient in a particular area, that is a surefire recipe for failure.

In Chapter 9, I talked extensively about how important it is to train and reinforce behaviors that are in line with your culture and values in a rigorous way. Just to be clear. This must not be confused with the training provided to all employees in order to foster a culture with a lasting impact. The training and development I'm referring to here are solely for the company's leaders and managers.

Internally, there should be a strong emphasis on leadership development that regularly addresses and enables company leaders and managers to enhance their leadership performance by developing key competencies. The problem with the vast number of leadership development programs is that they are scattered throughout an organization. In other words, training will only take place for a limited number of months each year, and it will not be open to all of the company's leaders and managers.

The goal should be to build a leadership factory that consistently develops all leaders and managers, where they in turn develop those they lead and create more leaders within the company. And, yes, this leadership development training takes place alongside the cultural and behavioral training mentioned in Chapter 9. To begin the process of creating a leadership factory, one must first adopt the proper frame of mind. Developing leaders and managers should be a top priority, and even business demands can't cause these efforts to be postponed or stopped.

Here's a great example of the frame of mind I'm referring to.

On February 26, 2009, all Starbucks locations were closed for three and a half hours, from 5:30 to 9:00 p.m., for barista training. The reason was that founder and CEO Howard Schultz had ordered it. Following a leave of absence, he had heard rumors that the company's baristas were no longer making delicious lattes. That was unacceptable, he believed. As a global behemoth, Schultz believed that the company had lost some of its "romance" and "soul." As a result, Schultz took action and returned to the main store himself, as well as quickly implementing an emergency training program in all of his stores.

Schultz could have simply issued a directive or delegated this task to another party. Instead, he acted as the organization's founder and leader. He personally got involved, his managers got involved, and finally every single store got involved. He set the standard. This had a ripple effect on the leaders of other Starbucks coffee shops around the world.

The goal of the massive barista work stoppage, which was explained in a memo, entitled "Transformation Agenda Communication #8," was to "teach, educate and share our love for coffee."

Ann-Marie Kurtz, Starbucks' Manager of Global Coffee and Tea education, said the measure would give "baristas the chance to really slow down and have the chance to really celebrate the art of espresso."

Starbucks' sales had been dwindling as McDonald's and Dunkin' Donuts increased their efforts in the marketplace. When Starbucks closed for emergency training, Dunkin' Donuts took advantage of the opportunity by offering 99-cent lattes and cappuccinos.

Schultz's leadership contributed to the company's recovery. At the time, Starbucks had 44 million weekly transactions, which was a testament to the company's strong leadership and the loyalty of its customers.[11]

As always, the ultimate differentiator is leadership, as exemplified by Howard Schultz, Starbucks' founder and CEO. Stopping operations for even a few hours across the country is a difficult task, but that is the type of precedent that must be set when it comes to leadership development.

Even though the Starbucks example wasn't solely focused on its leaders and managers and it was in a dire situation, it highlights the mindset needed to win, which is taking the time to develop and grow, even if it means temporarily suspending operations. Developing your company's leaders and managers should always be a top priority.

This serves as a reminder that, at the same rate as the world around us changes, the skillsets and competencies required of leaders to successfully lead their organizations into the future change as well. Who knows what might happen in the future to completely change business dynamics and how we work? We must be ready. More importantly, your leaders and managers must be ready.

What was effective and useful ten years ago is likely to be completely ineffective today, and what's effective today will most likely not be effective a few years from now. Building a leadership factory not only helps leaders excel at bringing the culture to life, but it also aids in succession planning, talent attraction, talent development, and even workplace fulfillment, among many other benefits.

There will always be a strong desire in any company to find and recruit new talented leaders to implement new processes and procedures. I've never worked with an organization where senior leaders weren't constantly on the lookout for potential leaders and high-performing managers to join them. It is critical to recruit and always be on the lookout for outside talent, but there should be an even stronger emphasis on developing current leaders and managers.

That is what an organization has direct control over. How well they train their current leaders and managers and/or whether or not it is ruthlessly prioritized, mean everything. When recruiting new talent, many variables come into play, some of which are beyond the organization's control.

Figure 10.3 is an outline of what we implemented at SGWS-IL to paint a clearer picture of the main objectives in building

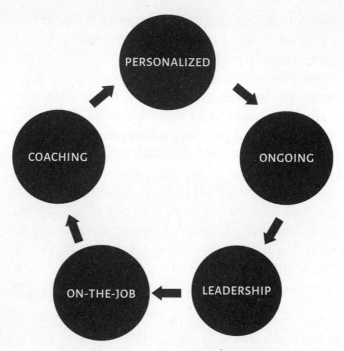

FIGURE 10.3 Five Key Elements to Leadership Development

a leadership factory and leadership development program to improve leadership performance and drive the business. The goal was to help more managers progress from good managers to great leaders while also continuing to develop even the most senior executives.

Five Key Elements to a Successful Leadership Development Program

The following are the five key elements for a company-wide initiative to aggressively upskill and develop all leaders and managers:

1. **Personalized:** Every program was tailored to help leaders develop the skills and competencies that were most important in driving commercial performance.

2. **Ongoing:** It was stated from the beginning that the training programs would be frequent, consistent, and ongoing. It would not be something that happened infrequently or would be disrupted during a particularly busy month or quarter.

3. **Leadership:** "Leadership in everything we do" was one of the FAMILY Values at SGWS-IL, so it was at the heart of every training initiative. Regardless of title or current rank, we wanted to develop leaders at all levels of the organization.

4. **On-the-job:** Conducting a monthly meeting or even planning an extensive training program all by itself is insufficient. For maximum impact, there must be a strong emphasis on on-the-job application. Every meeting, program, and training session included some sort of exercise that they could use in their daily roles.

5. **Coaching:** We not only wanted to instill a coaching mindset in all leaders and managers, but there were frequent reflection and coaching conversations highlighting everything that was introduced.

The outline of the leadership development program that was presented to the rest of the organization was overwhelming at first. As time passed and team members became accustomed to the cadence, it became something many leaders looked forward to. More importantly, the impact and outcomes were exceptional. Directors and managers were promoted at a rapid pace, and senior leaders actually started to transform into completely different leaders who exponentially improved their effectiveness in their specific role.

Although the primary goal of creating and implementing an extensive leadership development program was to cultivate leadership excellence, it also aided in steering and sustaining the culture. Leaders were better prepared to show up and communicate the culture, how it affected their role in the business, and, more importantly, to win the hearts and minds of those they led.

When the performance and skillset of an organization's leaders are maximized and improved, the culture will be positively affected, which will help enhance overall business performance.

Leadership Action Steps and Reminders

1. **Performance:** Never undervalue the importance of leaders and managers in shaping or changing culture. External factors may be unfavorable at times and contribute to the occurrence of a stumbling block, but at the end of the day, it all boils down to how well a company's leadership performs.

2. **Impact:** True leadership goes beyond a job title or a position in a company. True leadership is defined by the desire and ability to have a positive impact on the lives of others and help them in becoming a better version of themselves. There are people who have the title of boss but are far from being leaders. Others do not have the title of manager or leader, but they make an impact right where they are, and others respect and listen to them.

3. **Vision, lead, coach:** In building culture, the role of leaders at all levels is to set the vision, lead the way forward, and coach for excellence. Don't just tell people about your culture. Create a compelling story and articulate a clear path forward that connects people to not only being able to envision a bigger future but also the daily actions of the present moment. After the vision has been formed and communicated, lead the way. Leaders take the lead and go first. Weekly, ask yourself if you are modeling the behaviors you expect from others. Coach for cultural excellence. Ask your direct reports what you can do to help them in bringing the organization's culture to life. Actively listen and adjust as necessary.

4. **Commitment:** Become a transformational leader. Leaders must look in the mirror and evaluate whether they are changing and evolving themselves before they can change the mindsets and behaviors of others. Transformational leadership begins with a never-ending commitment to improve as a leader. The more you grow as a leader, the more likely

you are to begin transforming and inspiring others. The more people in the organization who are transformed and inspired, the more the culture begins to change. That is where organizational excellence is born.

5. **Leadership factory:** Make a strong effort to build a leadership factory. Don't leave it to chance. All leaders and managers should receive mandatory training on the skillsets and competencies that not only drive business performance but also directly influence the culture. Nothing is more important to your culture's overall success and impact than training leaders at all levels. When leadership performance improves at scale throughout an organization, everything benefits, particularly the culture.

6. **Implementation:** Make certain that leadership and management training is directly related to on-the-job implementation. An effective training and development program is one that is tailored specifically to close the leadership gap in the organization and encourages on-the-job adoption.

CHAPTER 11

Commercial Execution

I skate to where the puck is going to be, not where it has been.

—Wayne Gretzky, Hall of Fame hockey player

P eter F. Drucker, a well-known business management author and thinker, once said, "Culture eats strategy for breakfast." Well, yes, to some extent, I agree. There is power and significance in this quote. In contrast, I also respectfully *disagree*. I agree that if a company consistently devotes more time and effort to strategy while ignoring culture, the results will be minimal. I disagree because it can easily send the message that strategy is unimportant and reinforces the false narrative that leaders will be successful if they focus solely on culture while ignoring everything else.

This may come as a surprise, given the book's sole focus on culture and its importance. For many years, I used that quote in nearly all my keynote speeches, and to some extent, I still do. However, I'm more cautious about how I phrase it now because there have been too many examples of it sending the wrong message to leaders. "This isn't to diminish or minimize the importance of strategy, but when it comes to level of prioritization, culture is king because it determines how well you execute and bring your strategy to life," I always add when I use that quote today.

Although I am sure that not every leader interprets the quote in that way, one of the most common difficulties that leaders face when developing culture is its inability to drive commercial execution. In some cases, leaders believe that choosing between the two is even necessary because focusing on both is simply not an option. In all my travels around the world, the leaders who roll their eyes or believe that prioritizing culture is a waste of time are typically the same leaders who have had negative experiences when their cultures failed to deliver on strategy execution.

Creating a positive, inspiring, and meaningful workplace culture helps foster an environment where employees can grow and develop into their best selves. It is much easier for a company to retain and attract top talent when it has a fantastic culture. Organizations with a world-class culture have higher levels of employee well-being and fulfillment than organizations with toxic or stagnant cultures.

There is a plethora of other extraordinary things that prodigious cultures can do for an organization, and many of those things are discussed in this book. The sole purpose of an organization's culture, though, is to help drive winning behaviors to execute its strategy and achieve organizational excellence. Because of this, many positive outcomes can be obtained along the way. Such as an organization being recognized as a top workplace by local or national publications; profitability status reports; outstanding employee engagement survey results; or having fulfilled team members. As wonderful as these things are, they are not the primary driving forces behind what culture should perpetuate. Culture should and must be prioritized within any organization, but it should not be *separate* from strategy. Organizational outcomes improve dramatically when culture and strategy are intertwined and linked.

Let's return to the example of football coaches and how some of them are among the best builders of culture in our world today. Those coaches who are known for building renowned football programs and cultures and winning championships don't neglect the playbook and gameplan once they have an exemplary culture in place.

Their tenure as head coaches would be over in an instant if they spent all their time in press conferences publicly discussing the theory of culture while ignoring the "hands-on" playbook and strategy to win on game day. For these coaches, culture is the backbone of what makes their team special. They know that, in addition to culture, much rigor and time must be spent on their strategies and specific plays they will use on game day. Culture is the vehicle for cultivating and instilling winning mindsets and behaviors, while strategy is the gameplan for the point of attack.

The same is true in business. As important as culture is and the many wonderful things it can help an organization do both externally and internally, its sole purpose is to help that company win and drive commercial execution. When there isn't a strong and consistent focus on connecting culture and strategy, culture begins to be viewed as fluff that doesn't help drive the business forward. Culture should be one of the factors, if not the most important, in how well an organization executes its go-to-market strategy and improves its overall performance.

All the positive effects that circulate throughout an organization because of having a great workplace culture are extremely important and should never be discounted. However, they become minimized if performance suffers. Don't get me wrong: there is plenty of research and evidence to suggest that the happier an organization's employees are, the higher their productivity and performance will be.

You might ask yourself at this point:

- Did we cascade our strategic priorities from the highest hierarchical level to the lower levels, from one function to another? Are we also incorporating a bottoms-up approach to truly listen to our people?
- Have we made the right decision about which functions should be centralized and decentralized?
- Did we align the strategy throughout the business and engage all employees in our processes?
- Did we have high levels of teamwork and collaboration among employees, ensuring their fulfillment and the vital role they play in the company succeeding?

It was discovered in a six-month study conducted by the University of Oxford's Sad Business School in England that employees who were happy at work were also more productive each day. A survey asking employees to rate their happiness on a scale of "sad to very happy" was sent out each week via email. Researchers discovered that happy employees worked faster and made more calls per hour, resulting in a 13% increase in sales compared to unhappy employees.[1]

So, while making your people and employees happy is important and can have a significant impact on their job performance, it is not the primary driver of building a great culture. Many leaders and organizations struggle to build a culture that enhances commercial performance because they believe that the primary role of culture is to simply make people happy.

Things aren't made any easier by the multitude of opposing viewpoints that exist. One of the central tenets of labor unions and many progressive politicians is that employee happiness should be prioritized above all else. To make matters worse, many of the things that make employees happy, or so they believe, are perks such as unlimited vacation time, a willingness to resist workplace competition, the avoidance of conflict, and a growing resistance to internal change aimed at advancing the company. It's these very perks that prevent a company from delivering exceptional customer experiences and advancing and winning. These perks may make employees happy in the short term, but if the company isn't succeeding and fulfilling the overall mission of why the company exists, that happiness will eventually fade away.[2]

In his book, *Winning on Purpose*, author Fred Reichheld writes, "I argue that beyond competitive salaries and benefits, what makes a company a great place to work is when it puts workers in the position to do great things for customers. Building lives of meaning and purpose."

That is the power of creating a culture that is closely tied to the organization's strategy. It improves organizational performance and encourages employees to work with a sense of mission toward a greater good. While it's important to make our employees happy as leaders and managers, we must not lose sight of the broader picture of what culture needs to accomplish.

After laying a solid foundation, all leaders and managers must ensure that the culture of the organization is aligned with the commercial execution strategy. This chapter focuses on commercial success and organizational excellence. Now that you've set up a solid foundation and process for the ongoing growth of your culture, it's time to focus on results.

Keep the "Main Thing" the "Main Thing"

While working with an electrical company to help senior leaders implement their vision in an effort to greatly improve the company's culture, I noticed something wasn't quite right. During the first meeting, which was made up of senior leaders and another 200 employees from all levels of the company, there were a lot of different ideas and thoughts about the current culture.

In the weeks leading up to our first event in Philadelphia, the senior leadership team was under a lot of pressure. Three years earlier, the market had become more competitive, and the organization's performance had been deteriorating.

Prior to our first meeting, I conducted a series of one-on-one interviews with company executives and managers to better understand the root of the issue. It was stated by the company's top executives that the workforce lacked the desire or motivation to improve or change. Even before the decline, they had been thinking in this way for more than three years.

When I asked the top executives what they were doing to change the company's current culture, they said they had no idea where to begin.

Michael spoke up, "We've held plenty employee meetings, and many of us on the senior leadership team have spoken to the various divisions during these meetings and town halls, but I swear, Matt, nothing has worked."

Many of the company's employees whom I spoke with about the culture said the exact opposite when I asked what they thought about it. "Our current culture is amazing!" exclaimed Grace, a cheery administrative assistant.

What?!!???

This surprised me because the leaders usually tout the positive aspects of the workplace environment while the employees report the downfalls. So, what was going on? When I inquire about an organization's current culture, senior leaders and people managers usually say it's great, while team members embedded deeper in the organization say, "It can't possibly get any worse."

There weren't many examples like this, so I was curious to learn more before our first official company-wide meeting. I tried to get them to open up a little more by asking them more questions rather than just praising the culture. I kept digging.

Samantha, a manager in the finance department, confided, "When we tried to change our culture, we put a lot of emphasis on it five years ago, and there was a strong focus on improving survey scores and breaking down silos."

"What happened?" I asked. "Did you succeed?"

"Yes, I believe we did an excellent job on that front. But, along the way, we lost sight of what makes us special."

"Meaning?"

"We forgot what helped us in the past to become a market leader in this space."

This was an *Aha!* moment for me. Samantha's answer helped.

However, what I needed most came from Jim, a front-line manager who had only been with the company for a year. Jim had worked in a completely different industry before, but the company he came from was a powerhouse in their space. Jim wanted a change in his career, which prompted him to change jobs and move to a completely different industry.

When I had the chance to sit down with Jim, he said, "I really love the working environment here, but it has been a weird experience for me as everyone here thinks culture is about making people happy and giving them autonomy."

I nodded in agreement. It was obvious that the employees didn't fully grasp the significance of culture. Leaders also failed to link their culture to the strategy to drive results because they were too focused on meeting survey goals from both within and outside the organization.

Making people happy, survey scores, and meeting employee expectations are important, but so is ensuring that the culture is doing what it should: streamlining vision and operations, making the company more marketable, boosting productivity, increasing profitability, and ensuring the company's long-term viability. Those are just some of the possibilities. Depending on how an organization is currently doing and how healthy it is, it may be more practical at first to boost employee morale and strive to get small wins.

That's what the electrical company in the above example did five years ago. When they realized that morale and overall energy in the company needed to be improved, they acted at that time. They made significant improvements in key areas that were a source of concern for them, but the progress slowed over time. Once the basis of their cultural foundation was created, the leaders neglected to connect their culture to commercial execution. Unfortunately, this pattern went on for years.

By the time leaders noticed there was a major problem, the damage had already been done. People became accustomed to the new norm and accepted that "this is how things are going to be done around here from now on." After all, the survey results were positive. The mood was upbeat. Employees savored their independence. It bothered some that business performance was lacking, but there was a belief that it would magically improve in time.

Building a world-class organization in terms of health and performance should always be one of the primary missions and goals of the organization. But keep in mind that there's more to success than that. Being exceptional in one area while ignoring others will not ensure the organization's stability and long-term viability. A single pillar cannot support the entire structure indefinitely. For starters, it will deteriorate and fall apart over time. To keep it sturdy, it requires pillars on all four sides, but if they aren't taken care of, they will shrivel and crash down. These pillars focus on bridging the gap between strategy and execution to create a strong culture of getting important things done and soaring from one achievement to the next. This is exemplary commercial execution. It's all about keeping the "main thing" the "main thing."

Be Extraordinary

It takes extraordinary leaders (and people at all levels) to excel in a competitive business environment, and I've been fortunate to work with some of the best. Southern Glazer's Wine & Spirits is a prime example of commercial execution and excellence. At the state level in Illinois, I've shared examples and given an inside look at how they've changed the culture, but the excellence begins in Miami, where they're headquartered. They are one of

America's largest privately held companies, with operations in 44 states. Their level of consistency and complete dominance in becoming a category-leading enterprise are unparalleled, with annual revenues estimated to exceed $20 billion. That level of success and execution does not happen by accident.

John Wittig, Chief Commercial Officer, is an *extraordinary leader*. He has been one of the key driving forces behind SGWS's success and dominance over the years.

In order to create a winning culture that supports strategy and commercial execution, all leaders must improve their leadership performance, but it is even more critical that the leader in charge of commercial execution be one of the best leaders. John Wittig is exactly that for SGWS. You'll be hard pressed to find someone who says anything negative about John, no matter whom you talk to. His peers hold him in high regard and will be the first to tell you that his attention to detail when it comes to strategy and unleashing the full potential of others is unparalleled.

I was curious where his servant leadership mentality originated, because it was clear that this is who he was at his core. John is very deliberate in everything he does. When I asked him one day where he learned to be the type of leader he is, he replied: "I grew up in a military family and I am a teacher by trade. Early in my career, I realized that the command-and-control approach to leadership was ineffective. It's all about connecting the dots with what people need to be their best, and how I can help in some way to put the pieces together. That is what I tell every aspiring leader."[3]

SGWS's commercial success has been built on an extraordinary commitment from not only John, but also other senior leaders, followed by a laser focus on commercial execution and speed. Their remarkable success begins there, but it is not the only driver of SGWS's commitment to commercial execution and dominance. It is difficult to become a category-leading enterprise, but it is even more difficult to maintain this on a consistent basis and continuously outperform previous results. A big part of their continued success, according to John, is their ability to be innovative, futuristic-minded, and stay ahead of the curve.

SGWS, for example, prides itself on having the best data of anyone in the industry. Their quest to become industry leaders with the best data stemmed from the digital transformation of their e-commerce platform, SG Proof. In many ways, SG Proof's digital transformation was monumental, as it not only improved the customer and supplier experience, making orders more convenient, but also provided SGWS with key data to spot trends. The fact that SG Proof is proprietary is what makes it truly unique.

It would have been simple for SGWS to keep doing what they had always done. They have been enormously successful in becoming the nation's preeminent distributor of choice. Most leaders and organizations would have been tempted to continue as is, because the logical thought is, why fix something that isn't broken? However, given that two of their values are "Leadership in Everything We Do" and "Aspire to Excellence," it was critical that they incorporate those into their commercial strategy, to "practice what they preach."

It's great to talk about your culture and reward employees who embody your values, but if those values aren't linked to the commercial strategy and execution, your culture will rarely ever transform organizational performance.

Great leadership entails more than just leading others within your own organization; it also means having the courage to take bold risks and lead an entire industry into the future. To a place where the market will be in five years.

Hall of Fame hockey player Wayne Gretzky famously said, "I skate to where the puck is going to be, not where it has been." That's futuristic thinking. That's visionary thinking. That's looking ahead to see where you want to go and moving forward to get there.

"Complacency will always be the one thing that prevents most organizations from reaching their full potential," John explained.

In terms of one of their other values, aspiring to excellence means never allowing past achievements to dictate or direct future actions. Resting on laurels is not an option. Past success breeds complacency for many organizations and leaders. The late Andy Grove, one of the great management thinkers of our time and former co-founder of Intel, once said, "Only the paranoid will survive." Leading with too much fear and paranoia can quickly become a problem, but every great enterprise that is successful with commercial execution and achieves commercial excellence has a healthy dose of paranoia deeply rooted at their core. They are constantly asking themselves, "What if this happened?" and "How can we improve this?" An organization's strategic capabilities to execute and expand their vision to include what is possible can be advanced by adopting this futuristic type of mindset.

The first step to greatness is making the decision to be extraordinary. The best of the best know that complexity is the enemy of commercial execution and success, as well as the development of a high-performing organization. Being extraordinary entails not only developing a great culture but also exceeding expectations in terms of commercial performance and strategy execution. There is no choice between the two.

Find Your Commercial DNA

Researching great sports teams and incredibly successful companies is one of my favorite things in the world. I thoroughly enjoy learning about what distinguishes them from everyone else, even if others have more resources or superior talent. As a former athlete and now working alongside some of the most dominant companies, I've learned that the best teams all have one thing in common: They not only know what their unique DNA is, but they make full use of it. Even though they are in different realms, if you briefly analyze some of the best athletic programs over the last decade, you will easily be able to see that they used their strengths and uniqueness, their DNA, to their advantage.

The New England Patriots weren't always the flashiest team in football, and besides having two all-time greats in Tom Brady and Bill Belichick, their roster was not stacked with the highest-paid and most gifted players. However, because of their consistency in winning year in and year out, regardless of injuries or losing players to free agency, they were always in the mix of competing for a championship. They based their strategy on playing football with sound fundamentals, limiting mental errors, and capitalizing from the mistakes of their opponents. For the most part, they out-schemed, out-strategized, and out-executed their opponents.

Teams that have become well-known and left a lasting mark in their sports have each found and used their own unique genetic code.

Disney is another good example of incorporating their DNA into everything they do. I witnessed this first-hand as a child. I recall how excited I was the moment my family and I landed in Orlando and set foot on a Disney property. It wasn't necessarily because I was on vacation with my family or because I was able to see some of my favorite Disney characters, whom I idolized at one point in my life, although all of that played a factor. No, it was something deeper. Looking back on that time in my life, and even going to Disney now, it all makes sense to me. Disney understood its DNA, the "heart" of its business. It shows in the positive energy and emotional connection that the Disney staff creates and shares with the guests, as well as in the once-in-a-lifetime experiences that happen every second of every day there.

Walt Disney's unflinching and visionary dreams gave birth to one of the most successful corporations in the world. The Disney Company has done a better job than anyone else at understanding who they are, their cultural purpose, and their DNA to make dreams come true.

The six points below sum up the relationship between American culture and the organizational core and culture of The Walt Disney Company. These reflect American values, traditions, and customs and have recently been reflected globally in Tokyo Disney Resorts in Japan and Disneyland Paris in Chessy, France. This connection between Disney and American and international culture is a factor contributing to business success in the United States and internationally.[4]

Disney's global organizational culture and values, which reflect their visionary dreams for the world and the company's deep understanding of people and their emotional needs, include the following:

1. Innovation
2. Decency
3. Quality
4. Community
5. Storytelling
6. Optimism

These are reflected in a personal story from Kevin Brown, an author and speaker who is a good friend of mine. In his book, *Unleashing Your Hero,* he tells an incredible story about a family vacation he and his wife, Lisa, took with their autistic son, Josh, to Disney World a few years ago. What began as a routine breakfast with his family at Magic Kingdom turned into a life-changing experience not only for his son, but also for himself and his wife.[5]

Kevin's son, Josh, has dietary restrictions that must be communicated to the chefs whenever they dine out. The executive chef made her way over to Browns' table for breakfast that morning. When she arrived, she addressed Kevin's son directly, saying, "Good morning, Sunshine! My name is Bea. I understand we have someone on a special diet. How can I help?"

Chef Bea had been informed earlier by Kevin's wife, Lisa, that Josh was on a strict gluten-free diet.

Lisa continued to describe how she prepared and cooked recipes at home while Chef Bea listened attentively and took notes. After a few moments, Chef Bea posed additional questions to Lisa.

"What other gluten-free ingredients do you use at home? Where do you get that brand? How do you make that?"

Josh was ecstatic when Chef Bea finally turned to him and asked, "What is your favorite breakfast, Sunshine?"

Josh didn't have to ponder that for even a second. "Apple pancakes, please!"

"Oh, Sunshine, I am so sorry. I don't have the ingredients to make your apple pancakes special like your mom does," she said.

"I don't have the correct ingredients right now. How about some bacon and eggs with some special toast just for you?"

Josh agreed to the bacon and eggs breakfast with some special toast.

The next morning, at Josh's request, the Brown family returned to the same restaurant for breakfast.

Chef Bea emerged as the Brown family sat down. "What's for breakfast, Sunshine?" "Apple pancakes, please" Josh said wishfully to Chef Bea.

"You got it, my dear. No problem!"

The Brown family was taken aback. They assumed Chef Bea had forgotten about Josh's special diet.

Kevin, perplexed, inquired of Chef Bea, "Do you remember us from yesterday? You didn't have the ingredients for apple pancakes yesterday."

Bea explained, "I stopped on my way home and shopped for all of the gluten-free brands your wife told me about. You do know that we have grocery stores all over Florida, right? Anyone can go." She smiled mischievously.

Joshua beamed. He was going to get to have his favorite, apple pancakes!

The Brown family was pleasantly surprised. At first, they couldn't believe Chef Bea would have sent someone home from work to pick up the ingredients. When they learned that the executive chef went to the grocery store herself because that is what a customer requested, they were completely shocked. They had never heard of someone doing something like that before.

The Brown family ate breakfast with Chef Bea for the next seven mornings. It was the story of how one executive chef decided to show up and provide a once-in-a-lifetime experience of extreme care at her workplace for a single family. Talk about going above and beyond to please a customer!

Kevin shares this story all over the country to show how important it is to not be average and do whatever it takes to give people an extraordinary experience without expecting a reward in return.

Disney's distinct organizational and commercial DNA is at the "heart" of what they do, and it drives their commercial execution in the marketplace. Chef Bea knew how to "be extraordinary," and Disney is known as the most magical place on Earth because of their DNA, their culture. Because of their efforts to "be extraordinary." It can be seen in what they offer their customers and the rest of the world, as well as in how their employees conduct themselves on a daily basis. Disney's whole brand is based on providing guests with a one-of-a-kind experience that fosters optimism, happiness, and the vision to dream. That is not only advertised and highlighted in their brand messaging, but it is also delivered and acted upon in almost everything the company does.

Your organization can be visionary, too, in its commercial execution. It's inevitable that some aspects of your strategy and go-to-market plans will evolve over time as the world around us changes. Many of today's most powerful and well-known brands have retained some or all of their commercial DNA, even in a constantly evolving global marketplace.

The Seven Commandments of SGWS

During my conversation with John Wittig, he said that the ultimate foundation for SGWS's commercial success is still largely based on what is known as "The Seven Commandments of SGWS," which was created in 1970 by Harvey Chaplin, one of the original founders. Despite how much has changed and evolved since 1970, these seven commandments are still an important component of SGWS's culture and commercial dominance. The seven commandments are as follows:

1. **People:** Hire the best and pay them well.
2. **Relationships:** Never stop working with serving your suppliers and your customers.
3. **Branding:** Build wine and spirits brands on-premises, then aggressively grow them off-premises.
4. **Be innovative:** Always look for growth opportunities.
5. **Train, Train, Train:** There is absolutely no substitute for a well-trained sales force.

6. **Invest in Operations:** Invest in your operation and your back office.

7. **Invest in the future:** Be prepared to build your own "Field of Dreams."

Why is it so crucial to find your commercial DNA? Because, like the Patriots, Disney, and Southern Glazer's, it serves as a commercial compass for driving commercial execution, no matter how much the world around you changes. Discovering your commercial DNA simplifies things and keeps your focus on what makes you unique to drive commercial execution.

Market conditions and organizational goals for that quarter or year will change the direction of your strategy, but your commercial DNA is the unbreakable, strong core, the root, the beating heart. Commercial performance and results are transformed when they are combined with a healthy and high-performing culture that influences and inspires one another to guide the path forward.

Understand this: Every company has a commercial DNA. Whether that is currently being lived up to and executed in the market is another story. Every enterprise should do the internal work of figuring out what the DNA is and how it can be communicated and acted on in the pursuit of commercial execution and success.

An organization with a dynamic and great workplace culture is unquestionably a differentiator, and it can make all the difference in strategy and commercial execution.

Extreme Clarity and Understanding

John Wittig's unwavering commitment to communication is one of the most notable characteristics I've observed about him. And I'm not talking about just any kind of communication. I'm talking about detailed, in-depth communication on the SGWS commercial strategy and execution, with key strategic objectives clearly defined and embedded across multiple communication channels.

Every week, John sends out a newsletter titled "Commercial Huddle," in which key trends are shared with all regional and state leaders, followed by strategic objectives and revolving leadership lessons. This is not a simple email outlining the company's goals and direction. Instead, John explains the *why* and rationale behind his famous E3 axiom of Embed, Embrace, and Execute. The "Commercial Huddle" provides a roadmap and gameplan for how SGWS will win, where they need to dominate, and what all leaders in the company will need to do. Then, John's weekly newsletters are sent out, and leaders at the regional and state levels share and teach the information that John first shared.

When I first started receiving a few of John's weekly newsletters, I was astounded by the level of care and thought that went into each one. Then I wondered how John found the time every week to put this much effort into writing them, given the demands and rigors of his daily workload.

John shared the process with me.

Wayne Chaplin is the current CEO of SGWS. According to John, Wayne sets the direction of the company and lays out the gameplan for organizational success. Following that, John transforms Wayne's vision into a tactical roadmap for commercial execution, which is then communicated throughout the organization in a variety of ways. When I asked John about it, he replied, "We take pride in being world-class communicators. And it all begins with Wayne. He practices what he preaches. Everyone needs to understand where we are as an organization, where we need to go, and how we can get there as a team."

I spoke with ten different leaders from various SGWS states, and every single one of them said that staying on top of email is a daily challenge, but the one thing they look forward to each week is John's "Commercial Huddle" newsletter.

Just like we talked about how important it is to communicate your culture and what it stands for over and over again and never leave it up to chance, the same is true for commercial execution.

I've never understood leaders who feel compelled to keep the strategy and gameplan to themselves and never share them. *What good is that?* Each function in every organization has divisional and specific goals, but do employees understand the overarching strategy and how leaders arrived at that point? This is something I notice frequently. Senior leaders develop the strategy, and managers may be involved, but the vision and overall strategy are rarely shared widely. And that's not only the vision that's not shared but also the major organizational goals for the year.

How can an organization expect team members to be committed to the strategy if they don't know what it is, what they are working toward, and why?

The old and bureaucratic approach to keeping strategy and commercial objectives only at the top or taking a limited approach to cascading it is no longer appropriate. Not only does this derail performance and debilitate full commitment from employees, but it also highlights much larger underlying issues that could have a significant impact on the workplace environment. This is how an organization can easily undo all of its momentum and progress in efforts to build a better culture.

People not only desire and deserve to know what they are working toward but also need some insight into the bigger picture in order to clear up any confusion or misunderstandings.

The following are some considerations for what you should communicate in terms of commercial strategy and execution, as well as why it is important.

Commercial Vision and Theme

What is the year's aspirational vision for commercial success? Is there a theme or ethos that you can connect to that vision to make it easier and more memorable for everyone in the organization? For example, the theme for SGWS in 2022 was "FOCUS 2022." Each word represented a different aspect of their commercial strategy. Play around with yours, but don't overthink it. Maintain an unwavering commitment to sharing and spreading the commercial vision as it correlates with the vision of your culture.

Strategic Objectives

Whether you have three, five, or seven strategic objectives for the year, make it a priority to share them with the organization. Leaders and managers can then derive a deeper meaning from their daily responsibilities. This should not happen only once. It should be a regular, frequent update that shows where the organization is and tracks progress along the way.

Growth Pockets

How you won and experienced growth last year may have been completely different from what the market has in store for you this year. As a leadership team, it's critical to identify and communicate where the pockets of growth are in order to win that particular year. Broad statements or reminding others to be better than they were the previous year will not suffice. Communicating vague objectives will always yield vague results.

Tactical Roadmap

What is the tactical roadmap to help accelerate growth? This is your commercial strategy for winning and explains what needs to happen to drive the execution of your strategic objectives and growth pockets that have been identified.

Commercial Skills and Competencies

The breadth and depth of an organization's ability to identify and develop the most critical skills and competencies are almost always linked to its commercial success or failure. What are the skills and competencies that are directly related to the commercial strategy's achievement? This should not be a long list. Most likely, one to three key skills and competencies will be critical to adopt and implement in order to drive growth. Once you've identified them, they should be widely distributed.

Connection to Culture

It is vital to be able to articulate how your culture connects and plays a significant role in the execution of your commercial vision and strategy. Even if you have identified a few skills and competencies to achieve commercial growth, keep in mind that your culture is the vehicle that will get you from where you are to where you want to go. What role does your *Cultural Purpose Statement* play? Discuss your organization's values and how those behaviors, if lived daily, will pave the way forward.

Be Obsessed with Talent

The NFL is, first and foremost, a big money business. It's not like high school, where you get to play with your best friends with little care in the world. Even if you grew up admiring and loving the sport, in the NFL, it becomes a business above all else. Everything you do is calculated and analyzed in terms of talent and production, and if you aren't adding value or helping the team win, you will be gone in the blink of an eye. Furthermore, the coaching staff and front office spend every minute of every single day scouting college players and other players across the league to see who can be added to help the team win.

Outside of culture, the importance of being obsessed with talent was without a doubt my most important takeaway from my NFL career, which was brief and never took off as I had hoped or planned. Yes, the NFL is a highly competitive business. For many football fans, it's all too common to hear about players being traded at the end of their careers, regardless of how valuable they were to the team. Anger and dissatisfaction toward the team are common reactions among die-hard supporters.

I remember when Peyton Manning left the Colts. As a student at Indiana University, I had the opportunity to meet many Indianapolis Colts fans. Most Colts' fans I spoke to expressed shock and disbelief that management would do such a thing after Peyton had done so much for the team and the franchise.

As a fan, you have every right to be upset or angry; most loyal supporters are invested emotionally and often lose sight of the fact that this is a business.

There is a valuable lesson we can learn from the NFL as business leaders and managers and apply to our own organizations. Becoming completely obsessed with talent, constantly thinking about, coaching, and searching for the most effective ways to build talent. The best and most successful business leaders follow the model of an NFL head coach. Every week, there is discussion and thought about how to attract and retain top talent, maximize current talent potential, and ensure that the right people are in the right seats.

It is a huge mistake not to become obsessed with talent and to not put it at the top of the priority list for commercial growth. In the end, the level of market execution will largely depend on how skilled an organization's talent is as a whole and what skills and abilities its team members have.

Delegating the talent portion to the HR department is a common but costly mistake made by some leaders. Instead of delegating it completely, leaders should take firm ownership and work with HR and the talent development team in partnership.

NFL scouts who travel the country scouting college players aren't in charge of the entire talent process. They play an important role. They scout potential draft picks, analyze game film to determine each prospect's strengths and weaknesses, and then pass this information along to the coaches. The coaching staff and front office obviously pay attention to their scouting department and preliminary observations, but they have a significant stake in the talent process. Why? Because it all comes down to winning games and determining which players fit the mold of the current roster and can contribute right away, no matter how good the scouts are.

Coaches are the best judges of that. It's important to use the same logic in business as well. A business leader or manager knows which skills and competencies are most critical to achieving commercial success. Whoever is hired into the company and whoever joins your division's team has a significant impact on both the culture and the team's performance.

To delegate or not rigorously monitor and measure such a major matter is ludicrous. Not to mention that the challenges and complexities of the job market have made it more important over time to be obsessed with talent.

The best business leaders approach and prioritize talent in the same way that the best NFL coaches do. Horst Schulze, cofounder of the Ritz-Carlton Hotel Company, recently told me during a conversation that he personally performed every new hotel employee orientation.[6] In his book, *Excellence Wins*, he writes, "The most important thing a new employee can learn is not how to tighten a bolt or log into the network or find the first-aid kit on the wall. It is rather to grasp who we are, what our dreams are, and why we exist as an organization."

As a general rule, most leaders and managers delegate new employee orientation to HR. Can you imagine starting a new job and finding out that the COO and one of the cofounders are in charge of new hire orientation? As a result, it sends a powerful message throughout the company and sets a clear standard for new employees.

One CEO recently told me that he keeps a file that is constantly updated with potential new candidates for people he would like to hire in the future. However, being talent-obsessed entails more than just focusing on the hiring process.

It also includes a focus on continuous and constant feedback instead of relying on the annual review process. Most leaders find the annual review process to be ineffective, and it's not surprising. In a survey conducted by Deloitte, close to 60% of executives indicated that their company's performance management process did little to improve employee engagement and performance. Many of the most successful companies in their industry use a more realistic and effective approach: They hold real-time feedback and performance conversations with their employees following specific projects and initiatives.[7]

Relating to football, or any sport for that matter, if film were only viewed and analyzed at the end of the season, rather than after each game or practice, there would be very little growth and development. It is our responsibility as business leaders and managers to bring the same tenacity and focus to the organizations and people we lead and manage. The payoff will be enormous, but more than that, the growth and development of people are even more encouraging.

Commercial Execution Action Steps

1. **Keep the "Main Thing" the "Main Thing":** The primary duty and responsibility of culture are to drive commercial execution, which will contribute to an organization's overall success. Strive to make employees happy and do whatever it takes to create a positive work environment, but understand this is not the primary function of culture. Keep the "Main Thing" the "Main Thing."

2. **Commercial DNA:** Make sure that all leaders and people managers understand and embrace the company's core commercial DNA, which is the deeper essence of what makes your company unique. What is the factor that distinguishes your business from its competitors? Where and in what areas can you be the best in the world to facilitate the commercial execution of your strategy?

3. **Communicate:** Consistently communicate the commercial strategy, vision, and how it connects to your culture. Specify what is significant and what is not. Communicate how the culture and your Behavioral Manifesto can accelerate the execution of your strategy. Whether it's a newsletter like the "Commercial Huddle" that John Wittig wrote for his leaders and team, or some other method, if you fail to communicate, you will fail to drive commercial execution.

4. **Futuristic-Minded:** The world is rapidly evolving. You must conduct ongoing research to remain current on new market trends and innovative ways to exceed customer and client expectations. Resting on one's laurels is and will always be a losing tactic. *Where is the market headed? In five, ten, or fifteen years?* Reverse engineer and then focus on the process to accommodate the future.

5. **Talent Obsession:** You must be as obsessed with talent as NFL coaches and front office executives in the sports world. Collaborate with HR and establish a partnership, but do not delegate talent efforts entirely. The most effective and successful leaders are constantly exploring talent. Where they can find the best people, train, and improve the people they already have, and keep raising the bar.

6. **Be Extraordinary:** The standard is always going to be the standard. *Strive to become more.* Commercial excellence begins with the decision to become an extraordinary leader, to always go above and beyond, and to have a strong desire to execute and produce extraordinary results. Your leadership has a significant impact on your company, your people, and your future.

CHAPTER 12

Be a Chief Culture Driver

Whatever you do—whether you're a janitor or CEO—you can continually look at what you do and ask how it connects to other people, how it connects to the bigger picture, how it can be an expression of your deepest values.

—Amy Wrzesniewski, Yale Business Professor

M aking the decision to be *more* than just a leader or manager and to be a *Chief Culture Driver* encompasses so much more than just a firm hand and a strict agenda. However, when you are fanatical about your role as a *Chief Culture Driver*, it will be one of the best decisions of your career, regardless of where you currently sit in your organization or what rank or title you hold.

There is an immense opportunity right now for all leaders and managers to seize the moment and take the reins to create a world-class culture that brings out the best in everyone. When you truly embrace and intentionally implement *Culture Is the Way*, the future will undoubtedly be brighter and more successful than the past.

It's never too late for senior leaders who have just recently begun devoting time to culture-building within the last five or so years, or even if you haven't placed a strong emphasis on it yet. I meet and talk to senior executives who are nearing the end of their careers and planning to retire in the next few years, and who believe there is no point in becoming a *Chief Culture Driver* at this point. I assure them, just as I assure you, that there is no such thing as "too late."

Terry Brick of Southern Glazer's Wine and Spirits of Illinois (SGWS-IL) is living proof that it is never too late. Terry confided that he is nearing the end of his career, even though he shows no signs of slowing down. He didn't have to invest the time and energy that he did to build and improve SGWS-IL's culture, but he did, and that has made all the difference in the world in the company's remarkable success over the years. They have consistently grown their gross profit faster than revenue and revenue faster than volume.

What began as Terry taking a chance on trying something different from what he had always done by simply placing a strong emphasis on culture, turned into a transformative decision. "I may not have always been a big believer in culture, but I am a changed man," Terry said. "I don't have many regrets, but one of them is not devoting enough time and energy to culture earlier in my career. I'm so glad I didn't listen to that little negative voice in my head telling me it was too late at the start."

Here's the thing: When you make the decision to be a *Chief Culture Driver*, you're not just beginning the process of building a better organization or achieving better business results. You are also manifesting changes that will have a significant impact on how you lead and interact with others. This is the "humanity" factor. The "hearts and minds" factor. The "psychological safety" factor.

Even though Terry would tell you that he hasn't changed much as a leader, I beg to differ, and here are some notes from employees to back that up.

> *Terry Brick's leadership was outstanding throughout Covid and beyond.*

> *Terry has always been an approachable leader, but his leadership over the past few years has been truly remarkable. Empathetic, inspiring, and authentic come to mind when thinking of Terry.*

> *Things aren't always perfect, but I know we're in good hands with Terry leading the way.*

> *I must be honest. I thought this culture stuff would fade away, but Terry has done an outstanding job steering and exemplifying what Get Better Today . . . Together is all about!*

The decision of one veteran leader to decide that it was not too late to become a *Chief Culture Driver* had an impact not only on him, but also on those around him. It's never too late to start.

No matter how many years you might have left in your career as a leader or manager, being a *Chief Culture Driver* is and will continue to be one of your most valuable assets. Don't wait for the next crisis or hardship. Act NOW to take charge of developing and improving the culture of your team and company.

If you're just starting out in management or if you're an individual contributor who aspires to one day become a manager, becoming a *Chief Culture Driver* is essential. If you want to make a bigger impact and advance in your career, nothing can be more beneficial than learning how to drive and build a strong winning culture. Yes, you must execute and deliver results, but as we have discussed numerous times throughout this book, the role of culture is to accelerate growth and execution on an ongoing basis. Understanding the role of culture, as well as the common misunderstandings about it, will help tackle the misconception that it's nothing more than fluff with no real impact on business performance.

Every day, you must choose to be a *Chief Culture Driver* and lead by example. What transpired yesterday or a month ago is irrelevant. The only thing that matters now is that when you are given the opportunity to live another day, your feet hit the ground *running* in the morning and you don't stop. While running, don't forget the people responsible for making it all happen.

The Bigger Picture

Steven Spielberg's Academy Award-winning film *Schindler's List* was released on December 15, 1993. The film is based on the true story of Oskar Schindler, a German businessman who saved the lives of over a thousand Jews during the Holocaust.[1]

At the start of the film, Oskar Schindler, played by Liam Neeson, is a determined businessman who wants to make a fortune and succeed in business. It was Nazi law to encourage the exploitation of Jews as laborers, and Schindler took advantage of this at first. However, as time passed, there was an incredible shift that occurred. With the progression of World War II and as the fate of all Jews became increasingly clear, Schindler transformed from a greedy businessman to a truly courageous and inspirational leader. He began to see his Jewish workers as human beings, and he risked his life and fortune to turn his factory into a safe environment for all his Jewish employees.[2]

In the film, Holocaust survivor Itzhak Stern says, "Whoever saves one life, saves the world entire." In this true story, becoming a relentless, fanatical, and passionate *Chief Culture Driver* served a much larger purpose than simply creating a more successful business and high-performing organization. And now, the story of Oskar Schindler's courageous life and the powerful lessons he conveyed serve as a game-changing reminder for all leaders and people managers. Oskar Schindler used his factory as a safe haven for all Jews, which saved their lives. While we're not dealing with a life-or-death situation like Schindler, we can use this same mindset to create workplaces where all individuals are empowered to improve themselves and get better every day while doing work that energizes, challenges, and inspires them.

When Oskar Schindler changed his perspective from seeing Jews as *objects* to seeing them as *people*, he showed us how we should lead others as people first, and not just as employees.

The more your people—your leaders, managers, and employees—thrive, the more your business thrives. When your employees' lives are positively shaped and impacted as a result of where they work and with whom they work, the organization's performance increases.

Winning is and always will be of paramount importance. Just remember that what we usually associate with winning is only a small part of a much larger, more complex picture. Winning is about who we become in pursuit of victory, who we aspire others to be, and leaving things a little (or a lot!) better than they were the previous year.

As someone who has spent most of my life being labeled as a chronic overachiever, my perspective has shifted significantly over the years. I believed it was always the right decision to work harder and longer than everyone else. But as I grew older, I learned better.

Growing older inevitably brings with it a greater frequency of encounters with death, tragedy, and the suffering we see in the lives of those around us. And each of these in turn can easily influence our attitudes and beliefs. There is a greater understanding of the difference between the important and the insignificant.

I'm still a workaholic who believes in outworking others and preparing like my life depends on it, but I never lose sight of the bigger picture. Seeing the big picture can be extremely beneficial as leaders and managers, as well as in our personal lives when we return home to those we love.

Constantly striving and working to build a better culture has a broader meaning. Outside of delivering winning results and positive annual profits, there is a bigger picture formed of something deeper, something more. It's about humanity, the connection to others that will help all of us perform and even flourish. The irony of the bigger picture is that the more we focus on it and keep it in front of our minds, the better our results become.

As a leader, one of the greatest challenges is to step back and quiet the commotion and noise around you. Trying to sort out what's important and what is not can be extremely difficult, as can learning to stop and listen to the still, small voice within where our "connection" lies. Steven Spielberg, one of the greatest movie directors of all time, said the following about life and dreams:

> *If you have a dream, it often doesn't come at you screaming in your face, "This is who you are, this is who you must be for the rest of your life."*
>
> *Sometimes a dream almost whispers. And I've always said to my kids: the hardest thing to listen to—your instincts, your human personal intuition—always whispers; it never shouts. Very hard to hear.*
>
> *So, you have to, every day of your lives, be ready to hear what whispers in your ear. It very rarely shouts. And if you can listen to the whisper, and if it tickles your heart, and it's something you think you want to do for the rest of your life, then that is going to be what you do for the rest of your life, and we will benefit from everything you do.*[3]

The Magic Ingredient

Richard Branson, the business magnate and founder of The Virgin Group, once said, "Clients do not come first. Employees come first. If you take care of your employees, they will take care of the clients."

In business, the paradox is that many people want to win so badly that they obsess over hitting the number, deploying the strategy to drive execution, and running fast and wild in the process. Despite your desire to win, to hit your goals, and deliver exceptional results for your clients and customers, it's incredibly easy to forget that those are just outcomes. Having a great strategy does not translate into great strategy *execution*. A world-class product does not guarantee success on its own.

Great cultures don't just appear by accident; they take time and effort to cultivate from within. And that involves something more, something deeper than simply hard work and great ideas. It requires the heart of it all: People. That's the *Magic Ingredient*. That's what Oskar Schindler learned in World War II when he changed his perspective from seeing Jews as *objects* to seeing them as *people*. Schindler learned that there was a *Magic Ingredient* that was more important than profit and recognition.

Remember this: Who is responsible for hitting the numbers and making sure everything goes as planned? People are. Who is in charge of coming up with a winning strategy and then seeing it through to completion? People are. When it comes to product design as well as product marketing and sales, who is responsible? People are. Who makes up the culture of an organization? People do. Even with all the technological and AI advances that we have seen over the years, people are still at the center of nearly everything an organization does.

Even when you look beyond your own organization, where you lead and manage others, people are still on the receiving end of transactions when they're the customers. To win, you might sprint to the finish line as fast as you can while already obsessing over your next goal. You get so focused on achieving, doing, and winning that you lose sight of the *Magic Ingredient* that makes it possible to actually do those things. Your people are that *Magic Ingredient*. It's those people you lead, those within your organizations, and those tasked with delivering results and experiences to clients and customers.

The key to truly building a winning and world-class culture is to stay focused on the *Magic Ingredient*. Leading a people-first organization should be the primary focus of any leader or manager looking to improve or enhance their culture. This is more important than attempting to change the culture solely with products, slogans, internal initiatives, and a pleasant working environment. Putting people—your people, the people you lead—at the center of everything will pay off in a significant way.

Don't take my word for this. The research and data are fairly straightforward. In their attempts to achieve long-term success through internal transformation and change initiatives, about 75% of companies fall short. How can this be? Especially when most companies have a structured change office, a highly skilled transformation chief, and a strong desire for their efforts to succeed. One of these reasons, which is often the most prevalent, is that organizations spend most of their time putting their change agenda into action and rarely think about the people who will be responsible for making the change work.[4]

There are many strategies that can be used to change and improve a company's culture, which I have discussed in this book, but the results will be negatively affected if people are not central to any of these plans. The people must be first and foremost.

Leading a people-oriented, heart- and mind-oriented company, on the other hand, is far more difficult than it appears. It's more complicated than simply stating that employees will be given priority and come first. Your business culture only changes when the employees begin to behave differently because of your focus on their "hearts and minds."

Because of the rapid pace of business and the demands of daily life, the first assumption is to focus only on tactical implementation, execution, and results. I see this predicate in action on a daily basis. There will be a leadership or management meeting during which the importance of putting people first is empha-sized, and the next day, there will be leaders or people managers who have forgotten everything.

For those who are exceptionally motivated, there can be a natural desire to run faster, move more quickly, and encourage others to do the same when the pressure is on. One of the most important aspects of leading an organization that puts its people first is to never lose sight of who is ultimately responsible for get-ting the job done. That's the people, and that's the *Magic Ingredi-ent*. This can't just be talked about a few times a year. The senior leadership team, as well as all people managers, must prioritize and measure how they are actively putting a people-first organi-zation into practice on a regular basis.

What You Can Do Now

How does one lead and expand a people-centered organization in order to transform or change its culture? In other words, how should a leader implement the *Magic Ingredient* within the organ-ization? Here are some key areas to focus on that will not only help you build a people-centric organization but also increase the odds of changing and improving your culture for the better.

Ask Questions and Listen

Discard the PowerPoint slides or presentation deck and invite employee groups to a roundtable. Start by asking how employ-ees feel and how much change they can manage. Then, inquire about the issues they are facing. This is a good starting point. Next, pay close attention to the responses. Real progress is made when leaders and all people managers consistently seek to truly understand the mentality of their people, taking into account their energy, skills, environment, and workload. There is much more to encouraging and valuing employees than sim-ply checking a box.

Every business leader recognizes the significance and value of where financial capital is distributed, managed, and utilized. Every leader must also understand and distribute human capital with the same care and success as he or she distributes financial capital. Leaders who are aware of and understand their employees as well as their finances will be in a strong position to win.[5]

This may appear to be so simple, but it is often not practiced on a regular basis by leaders and managers. *Chief Culture Drivers* never pose questions for the sake of asking them. They ask probing questions to ascertain how their employees really feel, and then take massive action to meet those needs.

Redefine the Role of HR

I recently addressed 400 HR executives from across the state of Delaware at a conference. One of the main points of my presentation was to redefine HR's role in the organization. I emphasized that the one thing that is certain about the accelerated pace of business over the past few years is: All business leaders must change their perspective on the role of HR within their organizations, and HR's strategic support of actual business operations must be emphasized more. How quickly the half-life of skills is changing is a topic that needs to be discussed more actively within the four walls of every organization. The current half-life of skills has been reported to be between two and five years.[6] This is critical, because even if you have well-developed training and development programs, these will be rendered useless if they are not specifically designed to address the skills gap.

The active role HR leaders play in the business is a common barrier to an organization becoming a people-first organization where their talent capital becomes one of their greatest competitive advantages. HR leaders need to be more connected to the business, its leaders, and the organization's strategic needs than just being thought of as an HR business partner. Instead, they should be viewed as value-creators of a strategic business.

Larry Costello, former CHRO at PepsiCo, Campbell's, Trane, and Tyco, said: "Most traditional HR leaders think about process and programs, and in terms of HR, they don't let themselves get engaged in strategic initiatives. They haven't invited themselves to be battle-tested. It's not about building out an HR department. It's about building out an HR capability. It's not about having the best health plan or comp plan. It's about being aligned with the needs of the business."[7]

Organizations and their HR leaders should consider shifting their focus from "jobs" to "skills" as another important consideration. To make this shift, business units must move away from traditional job roles and align with specific skill profiles to match talent to open positions. When specific skills are the main focus, a much larger pool of qualified candidates becomes available. This change has a big effect on recruitment and attracting top-tier talent.[8]

Finally, redefining HR's role requires more than just changes from HR leaders. Business leaders must make a concerted effort to strengthen HR's relationship with the organization and to clarify its critical role. Do members of your HR leadership team attend strategic business and operational meetings? If not, that's a good place to start.

Measure the People-Related Stuff

Most great business leaders are obsessive about measuring every aspect of the business, every detail, and relentlessly tracking progress toward the company's main goals. There is usually a blank stare, however, when the question is switched and they are asked what people-related features, or in better terms, "the soft stuff," are measured.

Hopefully, by now, you've realized that the "soft stuff" isn't so soft after all, but rather essential to winning and becoming a category-leading enterprise. You may have wondered how to go about measuring culture and other people-related issues while reading this book. Maybe it was on your mind long before you opened it. One of the most frequent issues that leaders face when it comes to culture is the assumption that it is impossible to measure. Over the years, I've learned that it has less to do with the inability to measure it and more to do with the fact that many leaders don't measure culture or people-related issues as rigorously as other aspects of the business.

Your company's culture is just as important, if not more important, than any other critical business metric. Not only is it important to build a great, healthy, and high-performing culture, but it's also important to monitor and measure how well it's performing and being implemented. It's also not enough to rely on once-a-year employee engagement surveys. Not only is the frequency insufficient, but when culture and people-related aspects are measured only once throughout the year, feedback is rarely implemented. While it may be discussed for a few weeks, after that, it's back to business as usual.

The world's best and most successful companies frequently assess their company culture. For example, different groups of employees at Microsoft have a single question appear on their computers every single day. When they first started changing their culture, one of the questions employees were asked was how well the company's leaders were living the culture.[9] This is an excellent illustration of how the best of the best actively seek feedback and key metrics to help them improve and elevate their culture.

Regardless of the frequency you choose for your organization, make sure the feedback and measures you're receiving in terms of culture and people don't happen just once a year. Make it often and ongoing. When the pace and frequency of the organization and its senior leaders increase, it sends a powerful message to the rest of the organization. When that feedback and information are implemented, it sends an even stronger signal that this is not just a "check the box" procedure. A leader recently told me that employees despise surveys and don't need any more of them. Then, after he told me that, I decided to dig a little deeper and find out what the real issue was. It was no surprise when I learned why the employees despised the surveys. Senior leaders and managers rarely acted on what was shared with them, and most questions were never phrased in such a way that they revealed areas of opportunity and impact.

Survey fatigue is only a real thing when the rest of the organization and employees know that nothing will change in the weeks and months that follow. However, assessing culture and people-related issues in relation to business performance can still be a bit hazy for some leaders. Therefore, when it comes to enhancing employee satisfaction and the workplace environment, the most effective leaders focus on a few priority areas that have a significant impact on business results. They can keep track of progress more quickly and accurately when the focus area is condensed and there is a direct link to business outcomes.[10]

Putting It All Together

Being a *relentless, extraordinary Chief Culture Driver* will be the most important role of your career as a leader. There is one simple truth about you that I am aware of. You care. You care about winning, you care about the people you lead, and you care about improving your impact as a leader. You care about supporting the development of those in your organization and creating a winning culture. How do I know this? For one thing, you wouldn't have picked up this book if you didn't care. This tells me all I need to know about you as a leader. That you are committed to evolving, growing, and getting better.

The only thing I'm not so sure about you is what you'll do when you put this book down and go back to leading your organization, managing its daily operations, and taking care of your people. To put it another way, there is a big difference between what you read or learn and what you put into practice. Actions speak louder than words.

My greatest hope with this book is that you have been reminded of the critical importance of creating a great culture for your organization and your people, but that you also walked away with actionable ideas to execute.

In Chapter 5, I introduced the five steps to world-class culture-building. Every organization will be in a different place when it comes to constructing culture. There will be some organizations that may need to completely change their culture; some may need to improve specific aspects of it; and some may need to initiate a few cultural shifts to achieve greater market performance.

The five-step process can serve as a guiding light on your journey forward, whether you're trying to completely transform your culture or just improve or tweak certain aspects. Even though each of the five steps will have the most impact when carefully planned and carried out in tandem, your organization's needs and pain points may make it more justifiable to focus on one area over another.

Beginning in Chapter 6, I stressed the significance of developing a cultural purpose statement for your culture. This acts as a cultural North Star, defining what your culture is and what it stands for. If it is done right and not viewed as a cliché, the cultural purpose statement has tremendous power to bring the organization together and make it stronger.

In Chapter 7, I discussed a unique and collaborative approach to winning the hearts and minds of everyone in the organization. This stage of the process requires all senior leaders and people managers to actively listen to feedback in order to understand the employees' and company's strengths, weaknesses, and growth opportunities. This is the stage where a collaborative effort is made if a company desires to change or refine its values. This part has the potential to be extremely transformative, as everyone will have a hand in creating a better culture.

Chapter 8 was about creating a strategy to launch and implement your culture, which would help you bring about transformation and change on a large scale. At this point in the process, it is very important to spend enough time developing a communication strategy and a behavioral manifesto that connect core values to everyday actions.

The focus of Chapter 9 centered on being fanatical about establishing a long-term culture of impact and growth. In most cases, the excitement and momentum of an effort to change or build a better culture fade quickly. Building a sustainable culture necessitates fanaticism.

To build and improve culture, the final stage of the five-step process requires all leaders and people managers to lead the way forward and role-model the desired behaviors related to the values. The performance of the company's leaders is the ultimate differentiator not only in an organization's performance in the marketplace, but also in how well it manifests change and commercial execution along with transformation efforts.

In my years of working with and leading organizations through many cultural transformations, one of the most important lessons I've learned is to move urgently but to start small and slowly. As a new endeavor, there can be a great deal of excitement and enthusiasm but trying to change everything all at once can backfire. You can still operate with a strong sense of urgency, even if you begin small and slowly. From there, you can build momentum as time goes on, and you can accelerate exponentially from there.

A Final Note for You

What I've learned from working with leaders and people managers all over the world, as well as from writing this book, and what I hope you've learned as well, is that "no man is an island." We are on this Earth to live in harmony with one another, to work together, to serve one another humanely, and to give back to life in the best way possible. And we can't do it on our own.

On a personal note, I am aware that someday, in my final moments, before the light has left me—before my last breath—a deep rumbling in my body and the forefront of my mind will wonder if there was a reason for everything. To the phenomenon known as life. To my role as a leader who advises and coaches others on how to be more effective leaders and Chief Culture Drivers. Will I wonder if I've lived a good life? I'll want to know, feel, and believe that I did make a difference in the lives of others around the world, and I'll wonder, "Did you matter, Matt? Did you passionately teach and serve others? Did you give freely to others?"

And I will say, "I think so. I hope so."

This summary reminds me of a recent conversation I had with Horst Schulze, cofounder of The Ritz-Carlton Hotel Company and founder of Capella Hotel Group. Setting the standard for excellence, Horst led The Ritz-Carlton Hotel Company to become the first service-based organization to receive the prestigious Malcolm Baldrige National Quality Award. This incredible feat occurred not once, but twice.

Schulze is a legend and leader in the service industry, renowned for his vision of reshaping customer service concepts throughout the hospitality and service industries. In 1991, *HOTELS Magazine* recognized Schulze as the corporate hotelier of the world, and in 1995, he was awarded the Ishikawa Medal for his contributions to the quality movement. In 1999, he was given an honorary Doctor of Business Administration in Hospitality Management by Johnson & Wales University.[11]

In my discussion with Schulze, he explained: "Real leadership is *higher* than simply creating systems and programs. It's about people and purpose. And employees must understand the purpose and feel as though they belong. The company's purpose must encompass a *higher intent* because that's what creates excellence. And you cannot be an effective leader unless you have purpose, and you align that purpose with the employees of your organization."

He continued, "Communicate to your employees the purpose of the company—*the higher intent*—which can involve discussing the market's needs and customers' needs. And at the same time, explain how there is value in each and all of them individually, *personally*. People need to know that they matter."

Do more. Become more. Set the standard. Make a difference. Be a Chief Culture Driver.

Building an extraordinary, sustainable culture takes time, effort, and energy. It doesn't happen overnight, and it may not happen in six months or a year. And however long you believe it will take to completely transform or change your company's culture, add more time on top of that. The more challenging the journey, the more special and fulfilling it will be when you reach your destination.

True *Chief Culture Drivers* don't just wear the title with pride; they make it their full-time mission. There is no end date. Once you get started, it's a never-ending journey to create an environment that catapults the actions and behaviors that enrich the lives of your employees, customers, and anyone else who comes into contact with your company.

There is something magical about the human spirit when our hearts and minds become connected to a vision, a dream, or a desire that sets our world on fire.

Chief Culture Driver Pledge

My mission and commitment are to help leaders and managers of all levels ascend to the top and become *Chief Culture Drivers*. To make things easier for you, I've included an example of what I call the *Chief Culture Driver* pledge. As a reminder, some leaders have printed and framed this pledge, while others have written it on a notecard and carry it with them at all times. It serves as a daily reminder for leaders to refocus their attention on what is most important.

Whatever you choose to do with it, I am confident that if these words become your daily actions, and the actions of those you lead, you will be well on your way to building an organization for speed, impact, and excellence. And always remember, *Culture Is the Way!*

For Today . . .

For today, I will make the decision to become a Chief Culture Driver.

For today, I will do one thing to advance the culture within my team and the company.

For today, I will remind those that I lead that culture is how we behave, not what we say.

For today, I will echo the words that culture is our greatest competitive advantage.

For today, I will acknowledge one team member who exemplified the culture.

For today, I will encourage those I lead to impact the culture in one small way.

For today, I will have been a leader who showed up in a way that inspired others.

Notes

Chapter 1

1. Smith, Joe. "Coaching Titans Kerr, Maddon, Arians and Saban Talk 'Culture.'" *The Athletic*, June 24, 2021, https://theathletic.com/2647150/2021/06/24/championship-culture-real-or-overhyped-coaching-titans-kerr-maddon-arians-and-saban-weigh-in/
2. Clifton, Jim, and Jim Harter. *It's the Manager* (Washington, DC: Gallup Press, 2019).
3. Edelman. "2022 Edelman Trust Barometer." Accessed May 27, 2022, https://www.edelman.com/trust/2022-trust-barometer
4. Whitaker, Bill. "The Great Resignation: Why More Americans Are Quitting Their Jobs than Ever Before." *60 Minutes—CBS News*, January 10, 2022, https://www.cbsnews.com/news/great-resignation-60-minutes-2022-01-10/
5. Martins, Andrew. "Company Culture Matters to Workers." *Business News Daily*, December 1, 2021, https://www.businessnewsdaily.com/15206-company-culture-matters-to-workers.html
6. Beaudan, Eric, and Greg Smith. "Corporate Culture: Asset or Liability?" *Ivey Business Journal*, August 29, 2011, https://iveybusinessjournal.com/publication/corporate-culture-asset-or-liability/
7. Interview with the author.
8. Mirza, Beth. "Toxic Workplace Cultures Hurt Workers and Company Profits." SHRM, September 25, 2019, https://www.shrm.org/resourcesandtools/hr-topics/employee-relations/pages/toxic-workplace-culture-report.aspx
9. Clifton, Jim, and Jim Harter. *Wellbeing at Work* (Washington, DC: Gallup Press, 2021).

Chapter 2

1. The Sinclair Lab. "Welcome | The Sinclair Lab." https://sinclair. hms.harvard.edu/ Accessed May 29, 2022.
2. Clifton, Jim, and Jim Harter. *Wellbeing at Work* (Washington, DC: Gallup Press, 2021).

Chapter 3

1. Pressfield, Steven. *The War of Art* (New York: Warner Books, 2003).

Chapter 4

1. Wise, Jason. "Netflix Statistics 2022: How Many Subscribers Does Netflix Have?" *EarthWeb*, June 16, 2022, https://earthweb.com/ netflix-statistics/
2. "Netflix Gross Profit 2010–2022." *MacroTrends*, https://www. macrotrends.net/stocks/charts/NFLX/netflix/gross-profit Accessed June 22, 2022.
3. Dewar, Carolyn, Scott Keller, and Vikram Malhotra. *CEO Excellence* (New York: Scribner, 2022).
4. Gino, Francesca, and Bradley Staats. "Why Organizations Don't Learn." *Harvard Business Review*, November 1, 2015, https://hbr. org/2015/11/why-organizations-dont-learn
5. Gupta, Gaurav, and Rachel Rosenfeldt. "The Case for Change Leadership in Development Projects." Kotter, May 6, 2021, https://www. kotterinc.com/research-and-insights/development-projects/
6. Deloitte, "A New Twist to an Age Old Question: Does Culture Create a Leader, or Can a Leader Create Culture?" November 18, 2016, https://www2.deloitte.com/us/en/pages/human-capital/articles/ the-culture-or-the-leader.html

Chapter 5

1. Peters, Tom. *Excellence Now* (Chicago: Networlding Publishing, 2021).

Chapter 6

1. Samuels, Doug. "Mel Tucker Details the 'Relentless' Mindset He Demands of His Staff and Players." *Footballscoop*, March 17, 2022, https://footballscoop.com/news/mel-tucker-details-the-relentless-mindset-he-demands-of-his-staff-and-players
2. "Beyond Strength: Changing the Culture of Indiana Football." *Beyond Strength*, December 12, 2020, https://beyondstrength.net/2020/12/12/changing-the-culture-of-indiana-football/
3. Wertheim, Jon. "How Tom Allen Invigorated a Dormant Indiana Program." *Sports Illustrated*, August 24, 2021, https://www.si.com/college/2021/08/24/tom-allen-indiana-football-revival-daily-cover
4. Zeis, Patrick. "Nick Saban's Process: A Methodical Grind Towards Greatness." *Balanced Achievement*, January 19, 2018, https://www.balancedachievement.com/psychology/nick-sabans-process/
5. Gordon, Jon, and P. J. Fleck. *Row the Boat* (Hoboken, NJ: Wiley, 2021).

Chapter 7

1. Bariso, Justin. "Google Spent Years Studying Effective Teams. This Single Quality Contributed Most to Their Success." Inc.com, January 7, 2018, https://www.inc.com/justin-bariso/google-spent-years-studying-effective-teams-this-single-quality-contributed-most-to-their-success.html
2. Duhigg, Charles. "What Google Learned from Its Quest to Build the Perfect Team." *New York Times*, February 25, 2016, https://www.nytimes.com/2016/02/28/magazine/what-google-learned-from-its-quest-to-build-the-perfect-team.html
3. Edmonson, Amy. *The Fearless Organization* (Hoboken, NJ: Wiley, 2018).
4. Harter, Jim. "Employee Engagement on the Rise in the U.S." Gallup, August 26, 2018, https://news.gallup.com/poll/241649/employee-engagement-rise.aspx

Chapter 8

1. Clifton, Jim, and Jim Harter. *It's the Manager* (Washington, DC: Gallup Press, 2019).

Chapter 9

1. Gordon, Jon, Dan Britton and Jimmy Page, *One Word That Will Change Your Life* (Hoboken, NJ: Wiley, 2013).
2. SHRM. "In First Person: Satya Nadella." September 25, 2020, https://www.shrm.org/executive/resources/people-strategy-journal/fall2020/pages/in-first-person.aspx
3. Maxwell, John C. *Developing the Leader Within You* (London: Thomas Nelson, 2012).
4. Peters, Tom. *Excellence Now* (Chicago: Networlding Publishing, 2021).
5. Garton, Eric, and Michael Mankins. "Engaging Your Employees Is Good, but Don't Stop There." *Harvard Business Review*, December 9, 2015, https://hbr.org/2015/12/engaging-your-employees-is-good-but-dont-stop-there
6. Reichheld, Fred, Darci Darnell, and Maureen Burns. *Winning on Purpose* (Boston: Harvard Business Review Press, 2021).
7. Colvin, Geoff. "Great Job! How Yum Brands Uses Recognition to Build Teams and Get Results." *Fortune*, July 25, 2013, https://fortune.com/2013/07/25/great-job-how-yum-brands-uses-recognition-to-build-teams-and-get-results/
8. CNBC. "Power of Recognition: David Novak." May 11, 2016, https://www.cnbc.com/video/2016/05/11/power-of-recognition-david-novak.html.
9. Abbot, Lydia. "Q&A with Pfizer's L&D Leader Sean Hudson." LinkedIn, August 3, 2021, https://www.linkedin.com/business/learning/blog/learning-and-development/how-pfizer-is-using-learning-development-to-build-the-future-of-work

Chapter 10

1. Keller, Scott. "High-Performing Teams: A Timeless Leadership Topic." McKinsey & Company, June 28, 2017, https://www.mckinsey.com/business-functions/people-and-organizational-performance/our-insights/high-performing-teams-a-timeless-leadership-topic
2. Oltersdorf, Dan. "Better Results? Eat More Chicken. Interview with Dan Cathy, CEO at Chick-Fil-A." www.linkedin.com, 7 February 2018, https://www.linkedin.com/pulse/better-results-eat-more-chicken-interview-dan-cathy-ceo-oltersdorf
3. Yakola, Doug. "Ten Tips for Leading Companies Out of Crisis." McKinsey & Company, 14 March 2014, https://www.mckinsey.com/business-functions/strategy-and-corporate-finance/our-insights/ten-tips-for-leading-companies-out-of-crisis
4. Garry Ridge, interview with the author.
5. Ugochukwu, Chioma. "Transformational Leadership Theory." *Simply Psychology*, October 4, 2021, https://www.simplypsychology.org/what-is-transformational-leadership.html
6. Bass, Bernard M., and Ronald E. Riggio. *Transformational Leadership* (Hove: Psychology Press, 2005).
7. Schulze, Horst and Dean Merrill. *Excellence Wins* (Grand Rapids, MI: Zondervan, 2019).
8. Dweck, Carol S. *Mindset* (New York: Ballantine Books, 2007).
9. Dweck, Carol S. "What Having a Growth Mindset Actually Means." *Harvard Business Review*, January 13, 2016, https://hbr.org/2016/01/what-having-a-growth-mindset-actually-means
10. Kelly, Matthew, *The Dream Manager* (New York: Hyperion, 2008).
11. ABC News. "Starbucks Shut Down 3.5 Hours for Training." February 9, 2009, https://abcnews.go.com/WN/story?id=4350603&page=1

Chapter 11

1. Broom, Douglas. "Happy Employees Are More Productive, Research Shows." World Economic Forum. November 13, 2019, https://www.weforum.org/agenda/2019/11/happy-employees-more-productive

2. Reichheld, Fred, Darci Darnell, and Maureen Burns. *Winning on Purpose* (Boston: Harvard Business Review Press, 2022).

3. John Wittig, interview with the author.

4. Williams, Alex. "Disney's Organizational Culture for Excellent Entertainment." Panmore Institute. December 17, 2017, http://panmore.com/disney-organizational-culture-excellent-entertainment-analysis

5. Brown, Kevin D. *Unleashing Your Hero* (New York: HarperCollins Leadership, 2021).

6. Schulze, Horst and Dean Merrill. *Excellence Wins* (Grand Rapids, MI: Zondervan, 2019).

7. Charan, Ram, Dominic Barton, and Dennis Carey. *Talent Wins* (Boston: Harvard Business Review Press, 2018).

Chapter 12

1. Lowe, Lindsay. "*Schindler's List* Turns 25: Powerful Quotes from the Classic Drama." *Parade*, December 15, 2018, https://parade.com/724053/lindsaylowe/schindlers-list-turns-25-powerful-quotes-from-the-classic-drama/

2. "Evaluating Ethics and Leadership in *Schindler's List*—Humphrey Fellows at Cronkite School of Journalism and Mass Communication—ASU." Blog. February 26, 2013, https://cronkitehhh.jmc.asu.edu/blog/2013/02/evaluating-ethics-and-leadership-in-schindlers-list/

3. "Listen to the Whisper Speech from Steven Spielberg." Accessed June 18, 2022, https://esteemquotes.com/listen-to-the-whisper-speech-from-steven-spielberg.html

4. Messenböck, Reinhard, Michael Lutz, and Christoph Hilberath. "Challenges of Transformation – Putting People First." BCG, June 19, 2020, https://www.bcg.com/en-us/capabilities/business-transformation/change-management/putting-people-center-change

5. Charan, Ram, Dominic Barton, and Dennis Carey. *Talent Wins* (Boston: Harvard Business Review Press, 2018).

6. Deloitte United States. "The Future of Enterprise Demands a New Future of HR." Deloitte, December 11, 2018, https://www2.deloitte.com/us/en/pages/human-capital/articles/future-of-hr.html

7. Charan et al. *Talent Wins*.
8. Pearce, Jonathan, and Michael Griffiths. "4 Ways HR Leaders Can Reimagine the Great Resignation as an Opportunity." *HR Dive*, January 10, 2022, https://www.hrdive.com/news/4-ways-hr-leaders-can-reimagine-the-great-resignation-as-an-opportunity/616855/
9. Dewar, Carolyn, Scott Keller, and Vikram Malhotra. *CEO Excellence* (New York: Scribner, 2022).
10. Dewar et al. *CEO Excellence*.
11. Faith Driven Entrepreneur. "Horst Schulze & Faith Driven Entrepreneur." June 29, 2020, https://www.faithdrivenentrepreneur.org/bios/horst-schulze

About the Author

Matt Mayberry is an internationally acclaimed keynote speaker and one of the world's foremost thought leaders on leadership development and culture. His insights on leadership, culture, and business performance have appeared in publications such as *Forbes*, *Fortune*, *Business Insider*, *Entrepreneur*, NBC, ABC, Fox Business, and ESPN, to name but a few.

Global Gurus named him one of the world's Top 30 Leadership Thought Leaders, and his Leadership and Cultural Development Programs for organizations around the world were among the Top 10.

His clients include a diverse list of who's who in business with organizations like JP Morgan Chase, Allstate Insurance, Phillips 66, Ambit Energy, Southern Glazer's Wine & Spirits, OptumRx, Mack Trucks, Fifth Third Bank, Federal Bureau of Investigation, and WESCO.

Before becoming a sought-after keynote speaker and management consultant, Matt was a linebacker for his hometown team, the Chicago Bears. Due to an injury, Matt's career was cut short, but he learned invaluable lessons on leadership, culture, teamwork, and peak performance. By combining his experience as an athlete with his work as a consultant, working side by side in the trenches with leaders in every industry, Matt transforms some of the most prestigious organizations in the world. His real-world and practical strategies are impactful and actionable.

Index